The No-nonsense Guide to Training in Libraries

The No-nonsense Guide to Training in Libraries

Barbara Allan

facet publishing

Published by Facet Publishing
7 Ridgmount Street, London WC1E 7AE
www.facetpublishing.co.uk

Facet Publishing is wholly owned by CILIP: the Chartered
Institute of Library and Information Professionals.

British Library Cataloguing in Publication Data
A catalogue record for this book is available from the British
Library.

ISBN 978-1-85604-828-6

First published 2013

Text printed on FSC accredited material.

Typeset from author's files in 10/13 pt Revival 565 and
Frutiger by Facet Publishing Production
Printed and made in Great Britain by CPI Group (UK) Ltd,
Croydon, CR0 4YY.

Contents

Acknowledgements xi

1 Introduction 1
Introduction to this chapter 1
Introduction to the book..2
Contribution of training to library and information services 3
Benefits of training..4
The training cycle and the planning stage......................................5
The financial side of training 8
Legal issues..9
Structure of the book 9
Summary..12
References and additional resources 12

Part 1 Training practices **13**
2 Different approaches to learning and teaching...................**15**
Introduction 15
Three approaches to learning and teaching 16
A model for workplace learning programmes...............................21
Theories of learning..22
Bloom's Taxonomy of Learning...27
Levels of competence 28
Summary..30
Notes...31
References and additional resources 31

3 Making training interesting...**33**
Introduction 33
Action planning 33
Activities 35

Case studies 36
Demonstrations...37
Discussion groups...39
Drop-in sessions..40
Games 41
Group work 44
Guest speakers 45
Hands-on sessions 46
Ice-breakers 46
Inquiry-based learning..47
Lectures and presentations 49
Problem-based learning 51
Stories and metaphors..53
Surveys and questionnaires 54
Treasure hunts...55
Using a combination of methods..56
Summary...59
References and additional resources 59

4 Use of different technologies to support training practices....................61
Introduction 61
Apps...62
Audience response systems 63
Audio files 64
Blogs 65
Games 66
Interactive whiteboards...68
Mind mapping...68
Mobile learning...69
Podcasts 70
PowerPoint..71
QR codes 72
Screen recording 72
Screen sharing 74
Skype..74
Social networking tools 74
Surveys or questionnaires...74
Twitter 75
Videos 76
Virtual learning environments 76
Virtual talks 78
Virtual visitor 78

Web-based training 78
Web conferencing...81
Webinars...82
Web portals 83
Wikis 84
Summary..85
Notes..85
References and additional resources 85

5 **Making it happen** **89**
Introduction 89
Thinking about participants..90
Design principles...95
Designing face-to-face sessions...97
Impact of learning style preferences on training styles 99
Managing session timings 100
Evaluation of training..102
Marketing and promoting training programmes.........................107
Summary...110
References and additional resources 111

6 **Delivering face-to-face training sessions**...................................**113**
Introduction 113
Getting started...113
Different ways of involving everyone in the training process 115
Managing the learning process 116
Questions..117
Ending the learning process..118
Teaching large groups 119
Making database training interesting..124
Working with challenging learners 127
Summary...130
References and additional resources 130

7 **E-learning and blended learning**...**133**
Introduction 133
E-learning 133
Design of e-learning programmes 135
Web-based tutorials...135
Learning groups and communities 137
Blended learning..140
Design of blended learning programmes 141
E-tutoring 145

Evaluation of e-learning and blended learning.........................148
Summary...149
References and additional resources 150
Part 2 Learning in the workplace 151
  8 Learning and development in the workplace.......................153
Introduction 153
90+ approaches to learning and development in the workplace..........154
360 degree feedback 154
Accreditations 154
Action learning 155
Action planning 156
Analysing mistakes...156
Appraisal processes 156
Apps 157
Asking advice 157
Asking and answering questions 158
Audio recordings..159
Benchmarking 159
Blogs 160
Book reviews 160
Briefing papers..161
Briefing sessions 161
Cascade training...161
Celebrating success 161
Coaching...162
Communities of interest and practice 163
Competitions and prizes..164
Complaints..165
Conferences...165
Covering for holidays..165
Crises 166
Critical friend...167
Delegation...167
Demonstrations..168
Displays 168
E-bulletins...169
E-learning 169
Electronic mailing lists 169
E-mails..170
E-portfolio 171
Evaluating different products 172
Exchanges...172

Exhibitions 173
Exit interviews 173
External funding 173
Feedback..174
Fishbone diagram 175
Focus groups..176
Frequently asked questions 176
Gap year 177
Induction 178
Instructions 178
Internet...179
Interviews 179
Job rotation...180
Key performance indicators 181
Learning boxes 181
Learning contracts 182
Learning conversations..182
Learning journals 183
Meetings..184
Mentoring 184
Metaphors 186
Mind mapping..186
Networking 187
Online discussion groups 187
Online tutorials 188
Organizing events..188
Personal development planning 189
Personal development portfolios....................................190
Playing cards..191
Presentations..191
Professional journals..192
Professional organizations 192
Project work 193
Promotion..194
QR codes 194
Quality assurance activities 194
Quizzes 195
Reading...195
Reflection 195
Retreats or residentials 196
Rich pictures 197
Secondment..197

Self-assessment tools 197
Setting deadlines 198
Speed networking..199
Sticky notes..199
Study tours 199
SWOT analysis 200
Teamwork...201
Training a colleague 201
Twitter 201
Video clips 202
Visits...202
Wikis 202
Work-based learning qualifications..203
Work shadowing...204
Working parties..204
Writing..205
YouTube...206
Notes...206
References and additional resources 206

Index 209

Acknowledgements

I would like to thank all of those library and information workers who have had input to this book. This may have been through their participation in my workshops delivered at CILIP and other organizations, through their publications, websites and blogs, or by answering my e-mail enquiries. In particular, I would like to thank Anne Harding for her time and generosity in sharing her practice with me, and staff and students at the University of Westminster and the University of Hull who have influenced this work.

Earlier works of mine have helped to inform this book, including: *Developing Library and Information Staff through Work-based Learning* (Facet Publishing, 1999); *Training Skills for Information and Library Staff* (Facet Publishing, 2000); *E-learning and Teaching in Library and Information Services* (Facet Publishing, 2002); and *Blended Learning* (Facet Publishing, 2007). Writing this book has been an interesting process, as it has demonstrated to me that although there has been much change in training practice, particularly as a result of developments in internet-based technologies, the underpinning ideas and practice remain the same.

Thank you to Denis and Sarah, who have been patient and supportive during my time working on this book.

Barbara Allan

1

Introduction

Introduction to this chapter

The aim of this chapter is to introduce the context of training in library and information services. It begins with a general introduction to the aims and intended audience of this book, and some of the current issues faced by library trainers. This is followed by a section which looks at the links between training practice and the strategic goals and objectives of the library or information service. It is helpful for trainers to be aware of these connections, as the more effectively our training is aligned with the needs of the library and information service, the greater will be its contribution. It will also make it easier to access resources and support for training activities. The next section presents many of the benefits of training, and this is a useful list which may be edited as required by individual practitioners who are making a bid for training resources.

The training cycle is then outlined, and this involves four stages: planning, design, delivery and evaluation. This chapter considers the planning stage, and highlights the importance of working with a range of stakeholders to ensure that you develop an appropriate training plan (and one that meets the library and information service's strategic aims and objectives). Many library and information trainers become involved in training when they are asked to design and deliver specific training events or courses. These subjects, along with training evaluation, are dealt with in much greater depth elsewhere in this book.

There are a number of financial and legal issues associated with training, and so library and information trainers need to understand and follow their organization's policies and practices with respect to these subjects. In this chapter I have provided guidance on key themes and I recommend that individual trainers follow their own organization's practices and, as appropriate, obtain specialist advice. For independent and self-employed trainers, it is vital that you ensure that you develop effective financial practices, and your accountant will be able to advise you. In terms of legal advice, there are many government and other agencies that are able to help.

The chapter ends with a guide to the structure of this book and the content of each chapter. This is followed by a list of references and additional resource materials.

Introduction to the book

The aim of this book is to enable library and information workers to develop and deliver excellent training practice. The book provides guidance on the design and delivery of effective training courses and is aimed at helping experienced trainers, as well as those who are still developing their skills. It is a practical book which is aimed at library and information workers in all sectors who may be involved in training users, colleagues or other groups.

Individuals who may find this book of use include: library and information workers – public sector, private sector, voluntary organizations; learning, teaching and study support workers; knowledge workers; and library school students. Increasingly, library and information staff are being asked to do more and more with fewer resources. Training is often delivered by library managers, development officers and trainers who are on limited budgets and have access to few resources. Consequently, this 'no-nonsense guide' provides a straightforward and accessible guide to training practices and a wide range of tools and techniques which will suit different training contexts and situations.

The landscapes of library and information practice, including training, have been transformed in the last decade as a result of drivers such as rapid developments in information and communications technology, the move to a 24/7 culture, changing patterns of work and leisure, globalization, increased and changing expectations of stakeholders and the constant demand to work in a manner that is 'smart, lean and agile'. Training programmes are constantly changing and developing, and in recent years the growing interest in e-learning has expanded and shifted its focus so that many practitioners are now involved in developing and delivering blended learning programmes which integrate face-to-face and e-learning activities.

In the context of higher education and further education, library and information workers are often involved in training large, diverse groups of more than 100 students, often with very limited resources. In public libraries, library staff may be involved in delivering a wide range of training activities to extremely diverse groups. Many library and information workers in special libraries deliver end-user and specialist training to busy professionals who are unlikely to have the time to attend pre-scheduled workshops.

In addition, the rise of the so-called 'millennials' (individuals born between 1982 and 2002), who are adept at using social networking tools and other information and communication technologies, has meant that training practices are continually changing to meet their expectations as they move from school to college or university and the workplace. Langan (2011) summarizes some additional characteristics of the millennium generation as: having respect for authority but not necessarily for social hierarchies; being socially ambitious; and being unaware of their own lack of skills. The latter feature has implications for library and information trainers. According to Smith and Baker (2011), the millennium generation, as well as being very comfortable with technology, prefer teamwork and experiential learning, and they expect services to be available 24/7 in a variety of modes (face-to-face and online) with a quick response time. In addition, they are apparently more likely to use online resources than to visit the library. The millennium generation are also called 'digital natives' (Prensky, 2001), and this name is linked to the idea of individuals who have grown up with a diverse range of ever-evolving technologies which they use in their social lives, for e-commerce, for study and for work. One of the consequences of this millennium generation, who are now joining the library and information profession, as well as using the services, is that they demand a different type of training programme to meet their needs and expectations.

Working in these challenging times has led many library and information workers to develop a range of effective and innovative blended-learning training programmes which include: face-to-face events; drop-in workshops; online training; and the use of social media. They have developed the necessary skills by adapting and using new technologies such as Web 2.0 tools and Skype. This book provides guidance, based on current best practice, to help library and information workers to be successful in their delivery of training.

Contribution of training to library and information services

Most organizations produce a strategic plan at regular intervals, and these plans identify the vision, mission and values of the organization, as well as its main aims and strategic objectives. These plans may be developed in a variety of ways, e.g. top-down, bottom-up or through an extensive consultation process which involves a mixture of top-down and bottom-up activities and processes. The organization's strategic plan may then be used by the library and information managers to write the library and information service's strategic plan.

The strategic aims and objectives of the library or information service will be aligned to and clearly contribute to the parent organization's own strategic plan. The training activities then need to support the strategic aims and objectives of the library or information service. There are a number of reasons why training activities need to be aligned with the library and information service's strategic aims and objectives. The first is that *all* activities need to be aligned to the strategic plan so as to ensure that the library and information service achieves its goals and objectives. This is particularly important when there are limited resources, because the resources that are available need to be focused on helping the library to achieve its goals. If the library or information service does not achieve its goals, then its future may be in jeopardy. The second reason is that the strategic plan is a way of identifying priorities; the priorities of the library and information service are the same as those of the parent organization, and the training activities serve these priorities. The third reason is that aligning the training programme with the strategic plan is a way of demonstrating to stakeholders that the library and information service is supporting the current priorities and activities of the organization.

In large libraries where there is a significant training and development department, this department may write its own strategic plan as a sub-set of the library and information service's plan. Alternatively, the training and development plan may be integrated into the wider library and information service plan. These strategic plans are important, as they identify aims and objectives and priorities. Financial support is likely to follow the strategic plan, and activities that are not aligned with the strategic plan are unlikely to be supported.

TIP FOR TRAINERS

Read your organization's and/or library and information service's strategic plan. What are the implications for your training activities? What should you be focusing on? Which activities or areas of activity need to grow? Which activities or areas of activity need to be reduced?

Benefits of training

Training provides benefits for different stakeholders and it is often useful to consider these and present them to stakeholders when designing and developing training courses. The following lists of common benefits of training provide a set of headings (they may be expanded to fit particular contexts) which may be used to help in compiling a training proposal.

Benefits for the library and information service:

- increased productivity
- improved quality of work
- improved customer service
- development of a flexible workforce
- reduction in staff turnover
- reduced employee turnover, due to better supervision and management following leadership training
- reduced employee turnover, due to greater job satisfaction
- reduced recruitment costs, due to greater job satisfaction
- reduced recruitment costs, due to reduced turnover.

Benefits for staff who receive training:

- fewer errors

- correct implementation of policies and procedures
- improved knowledge and skills
- better quality of customer service
- saving of time through more effective use of systems
- increased productivity of new staff, due to effective induction training
- increased professionalism
- improved morale
- continuous professional development.

Benefits for customers:

- improved knowledge and skills
- improved performance through access to better quality of information
- increased satisfaction with the library and information service
- improved use of information and communications technologies
- saving of time through effective use of services and resources.

Putting figures on these benefits is very challenging. Here are some examples of the ways in which some trainers have attempted to demonstrate the benefits of their training events:

> I work in a research library in the construction industry. One of my customers came and thanked me for teaching him how to use one of the databases. He was able to find information about a particular type of building defect. He said it has saved the company about £20,000. I asked him to put it in writing and used this to help demonstrate the benefit of training.
>
> Information officer with a remit for training

> Each year, the National Student Survey is used by universities in the UK to identify areas for improvement. This year, a number of different students in different faculties commented on how useful they found the workshop 'Finding information for your dissertation'. The senior managers in the library and university were thrilled – this information is widely available and it really demonstrated the value of our training sessions.
>
> Academic liaison librarian

The training cycle and the planning stage

Figure 1.1 illustrates the training cycle and indicates that it is made up of four stages: planning, designing, delivery and evaluation. This section is concerned with the planning stage, which is sometimes carried out by specialist training departments or library managers. Individual trainers are often involved in training at the next stages: design, which is covered in Chapters 5 and 6 (face-to-face sessions) and Chapter 7 (e-learning and blended learning); delivery, covered in Chapters 5 and 6 (face-to-face); and evaluation, covered in Chapters 5 and 7.

The rapidly changing external environment means that training needs are constantly evolving. Training needs arise from the need to:

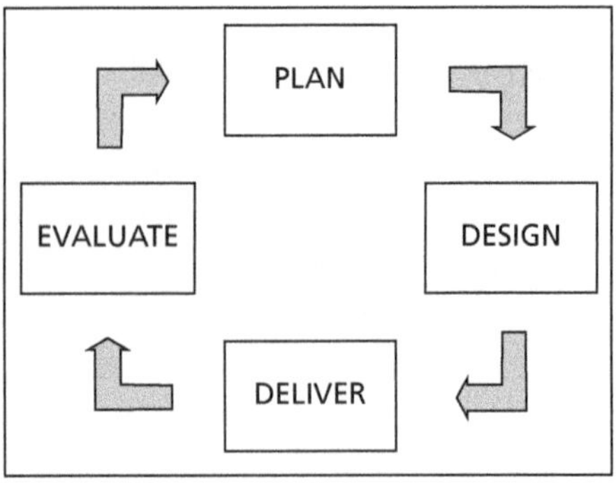

Figure 1.1 *Training cycle*

- bridge the gap between present and desired performance. For example, improving the usage of databases by ensuring that colleagues have more detailed knowledge of and skills in their use.
- improve performance so as to achieve continually rising standards. For example, ensuring that all customer service staff use all the features and functions of the catalogue system. Another example is related to the introduction of new systems, e.g. self-service systems, as a means of improving the quality of the service.
- do new and different things. For example, introducing new systems and services based on new, web-based tools and technologies.

The start of the planning process involves establishing training needs by identifying the needs of the library and information service, of the staff and of the customers. At the level of the library and information service this may involve looking at:

- the strategic plan – where is the library going? What are the priorities?
- key performance indicators (KPIs) – what areas do we need to focus on and improve?
- feedback from quality assurance processes, customer surveys and other feedback mechanisms – what areas do we need to focus on and improve?
- the capacity for training – how much resource (people, time, money) can we invest in training?

Identifying staff needs may involve:

- looking at the outcomes of appraisal or performance management processes – what training is required?
- asking the staff themselves – what training do you think you need?
- asking team leaders and managers – what training do you think the staff need?
- looking at feedback from quality assurance processes, customer surveys and other feedback mechanisms – where do we need to focus staff training?

Identifying customer needs may involve:

- asking the customers themselves – what training do you think you need?
- asking staff who work on the front line (help desks, virtual reference services, etc.) – what training do you think customers need?
- looking at feedback from quality assurance processes, customer surveys and other feedback mechanisms – where do we need to focus customer training?

In addition to using working documents, this process of identifying training needs requires research and it is likely to involve interviewing the following people:

- senior managers
- middle managers and team leaders
- internal customers
- external customers
- intended training participants
- other interested stakeholders.

The consultation process may involve asking a few basic questions:

1 What do you think should be the main aims and objectives of the training activity?
2 What do you want us to achieve in our training activity?
3 Who do you think should be involved in the training programmes?
4 What difference do you want us to make to the working of the organization/department?
5 How would you judge success in our training activities?

The information collected during the training needs analysis will inform the development of a training plan, which may include the following:

- overall aims of the training plan
- rationale and link with strategic plan(s)
- main objectives of the training plan
- main KPIs
- approach(es) to learning and development to be used, e.g. main areas of activity, types of activities (face-to-face training, coaching, e-learning or blended learning, workplace learning)
- indication of who will be involved, e.g. trainers (internal or external); who will be the participants; links with stakeholders, e.g. managers and leaders across the organization
- indication of the cost of the training activity.

The training plan will need to be approved by senior library and information staff, and possibly by senior staff within the parent organization.

The financial side of training

How do you cost a training event? The basic cost of any training event is based upon:

- number of participants – different events will be costed in different ways. In some, the participants will pay to attend the event. In others, the cost of the participants' time must be taken into account
- cost of the trainer's time – an external trainer will charge a fee. For internal trainers, their cost can be calculated using a standard equation (see Table 1.1)
- cost of travel and subsistence
- venue – the cost of using an external venue such as a hotel. However, using in-house space has a cost associated with it too
- technology requirements – an external venue such as a hotel will charge for the use of its technical facilities. However, using in-house technology also has a cost associated with it
- learning resources – the cost (staff time) to prepare and then reproduce or distribute them
- promotion – the cost (staff time) to prepare and then disseminate the information
- administration – the cost (staff time) involved in administering the event.

The main cost of any training activity is staff time. Many organizations have standard procedures for calculating staff time. If you need to calculate this for yourself, the equations presented in Table 1.1 can be used to calculate the cost of staff time for attending an event.

Table 1.1 *Useful equations for costing staff time*
Calculate the daily rate of staff using the following two equations:
Daily rate = (annual salary + on-costs)/days
where
days = working days per year – (annual leave + weekends + statutory days + sick leave)
Calculate the cost for each participant in the training using the following two equations:
Daily rate/number of hours worked per day = hourly rate
Cost of one person = hourly rate x number of hours of training event
Total cost of staff time involved in attending training event =
Sum of costs of each participant
Total cost of trainer time =
Daily rate of trainer x number of days worked on training event (preparation, delivery and follow-up activities)

Legal issues

It is important to be aware of some of the legal issues associated with training and to have a general understanding of the following topics (if they are applicable to your training practice):

- child protection (for individuals working with children)
- copyright and intellectual property
- corporate manslaughter
- data protection
- disability issues
- freedom of information
- health and safety
- employer's liability insurance.

This list isn't meant to be scary, but it does demonstrate that there are a variety of legal issues relevant to training. It is beyond the scope of this book to provide legal guidance and, if in doubt, you should obtain advice from your manager or a relevant specialist or solicitor within your own organization. Typical situations that occur in training practice include:

- the need for the trainer to ensure that the training environment is safe. If in doubt, contact the appropriate health and safety officer
- the need to obtain written permission to use other people's training materials or resources
- the need to comply with data protection law and not to provide personal information to a third party
- the need to make reasonable adjustments for individuals with a disability who are attending the training event.

For independent, freelance or self-employed trainers it is vital to have professional indemnity insurance (called errors and omissions, E&O, in the USA), as this helps to provide protection in terms of potential litigation relating to the provision of incorrect information or advice, or a claim of negligence. It is often possible to obtain this type of insurance via a professional association (which may offer a discount on premiums) as well as through insurance companies.

Structure of the book

This book is divided into two parts: Part 1 is concerned with training practice, i.e. planning, designing and delivering training events, including e-learning and blended learning programmes; Part 2 is concerned with learning in the workplace. It offers more than 90 approaches to developing learning activities in the workplace.

Part 1 begins with Chapter 2, which considers different approaches to learning and teaching. It starts by exploring three main approaches: content or trainer centred, where the focus is on what is to be taught; student centred, which, as the name implies, put students or learners at the centre of the learning process; and finally social approaches. Social approaches to learning are particularly relevant in continuous professional development, where formal or informal learning communities are often developed as part of the training strategy. Currently, there is a shift in training in the workplace to designing development programmes which are integrated into workplace practices. This is the so-called 70:20:10 model, which is explored in the chapter. Finally, Chapter 2 ends with an exploration of three different models of learning styles and their relevance to training; of Bloom's Taxonomy of Learning; and of the Learning Competences model. These learning theories have been selected as they are extremely relevant to training practice in a variety of contexts.

Chapter 3 is concerned with making training interesting, i.e. using a range of learning and teaching methods, and it looks at a number of standard training methods:

- action planning
- activities
- case studies
- demonstrations
- discussion groups
- drop-in sessions
- games
- group work
- guest speakers
- hands-on sessions
- ice-breakers
- inquiry-based learning
- lectures and presentations
- problem-based learning
- stories and metaphors
- surveys and questionnaires
- treasure hunts.

These methods have been selected because they cover many of the standard training practices in library and information work. There are other approaches to learning and training, and many of them are described in Part 2 of this book.

Chapter 4 focuses on using a range of technologies to support training practice. One of the challenges of writing this chapter has been the speed of change and the continuing availability of new tools and techniques to help support training activities. Consequently, the chapter focuses on providing a general overview of the different ways in which current technologies may be incorporated into training programmes. It covers a range of ICTs (information and communication technologies) in some detail.

Chapter 5 is about 'making it happen', which involves knowing your learners and their needs. The chapter includes sections on: design principles; evaluation of training; and marketing and promoting training events. Although the design principles relate to all types of training (face-to-face, e-learning and blended learning), the main focus of this chapter is the design and evaluation of face-to-face training. E-learning and blended learning are considered in more detail in Chapter 7.

Delivering face-to-face training is the focus of Chapter 6, which is concerned with the practical aspects of running training sessions, including: getting started; managing the learning process; dealing with questions; ending the training sessions. A number of common training situations are explored in some detail, with a focus on teaching large groups and making database training interesting.

E-learning and blended learning run as a theme throughout all the chapters, but are dealt with as a separate topic in Chapter 7. This provides an opportunity to explore these two approaches to training in more detail and to consider how to design, deliver and evaluate such programmes. There is also a section which considers the skills required by e-tutors.

Part 2 of this book consists wholly of Chapter 8, which offers an exploration of over 90 approaches to learning in the workplace (Table 1.2). This chapter is

Table 1.2 *90+ approaches to work-place learning*

1	360 degree feedback	35	Exchanges	66	Professional journals
2	Accreditations	36	Exhibitions	67	Professional
3	Action learning	37	Exit interviews		organizations
4	Action planning	38	External funding	68	Project work
5	Analysing mistakes	39	Feedback	69	Promotion
6	Appraisal processes	40	Fishbone diagram	70	QR codes
7	Apps	41	Focus groups	71	Quality assurance
8	Asking advice	42	Frequently asked		activities
9	Asking and answering		questions	72	Quizzes
	questions	43	Gap year	73	Reading
10	Audio recordings	44	Induction	74	Reflection
11	Benchmarking	45	Instructions	75	Retreats or residentials
12	Blogs	46	Internet	76	Rich pictures
13	Book reviews	47	Interviews	77	Secondment
14	Briefing papers	48	Job rotation	78	Self-assessment tools
15	Briefing sessions	49	Key performance	79	Setting deadlines
16	Cascade training		indicators	80	Speed networking
17	Celebrating success	50	Learning boxes	81	Sticky notes
18	Coaching	51	Learning contracts	82	Study tours
19	Communities of interest	52	Learning conversations	83	SWOT analysis
20	Competitions and prizes	53	Learning journals	84	Teamwork
21	Complaints	54	Meetings	85	Training a colleague
22	Conferences	55	Mentoring	86	Twitter
23	Covering for holidays	56	Metaphors	87	Video clips
24	Crises	57	Mind mapping	88	Visits
25	Critical friend	58	Networking	89	Wikis
26	Delegation	59	Online discussion	90	Work-based learning
27	Demonstrations		groups		qualifications
28	Displays	60	Online tutorials	91	Work shadowing
29	E-bulletins	61	Organizing events	92	Working parties
30	E-learning	62	Personal development	93	Writing
31	Electronic mailing lists		planning	94	YouTube
32	E-mails	63	Personal development		
33	E-portfolio		portfolios		
34	Evaluating different	64	Playing cards		
	products	65	Presentations		

included because training budgets and resources to enable individuals to attend training events are increasingly tight. This means that workplace learning is becoming very important, and a popular model is the 70:20:10 framework (see Chapter 2). The basic idea behind the 70:20:10 framework is that 70% of learning takes place in the workplace by means of dealing with challenging activities; 20% involves learning from colleagues; and 10% is based on courses and reading. This section is integral to the book, as it helps to promote a wide range of activities for workplace learning, which it is hoped will offer inspiration to readers of this book to develop these ideas in their places of work.

Summary

The aim of this chapter has been to introduce the reader to this book and to the current context for training practices in library and information services. This has included a discussion on the contribution of training to the achievements of library and information services, and the importance of aligning training and development practices to strategic aims and objectives, which enables training to make an impact on the organization and its staff and stakeholders. This was followed by an introduction to the four-stage training cycle (planning, designing, delivery and evaluation) and an outline of the initial planning stage. The two important areas of financial and legal issues in training were then brought into play. This book is divided into two parts, Part 1: Training Practices and Part 2: Learning in the Workplace, and the remainder of Chapter 1 provided an outline of the content and focus of each chapter, enabling the reader to identify their starting point for either working through the whole book or dipping into relevant sections as desired.

References and additional resources

Cornish, G. (2009) *Copyright: interpreting the law for libraries, archives and information services*, 5th edn, Facet Publishing.

Hales, A. and Atwell, B. (nyp) *The No-nonsense Guide to Copyright in All Media*, Facet Publishing.

Langan, K. (2011) Training Millennials: a practical and theoretical approach, *Reference Services Review*, **40** (1), 24–48.

Oppenheim, C. (2012) *The No-nonsense Guide to Legal Issues in Web 2.0 and Cloud Computing*, Facet Publishing.

Pedley, P. (2012) *The E-copyright Handbook*, Facet Publishing.

Prensky, M. (2001) Digital Natives, Digital Immigrants, *On the Horizon*, 9 (5), 1–6.

Secker, J. (2010) *Copyright and E-learning: a guide for practitioners*, Facet Publishing.

Smith, A.-L. and Baker, L. (2011) Getting a Clue: creating student detectives and dragon slayers in your library, *Reference Services Review*, **39** (4), 628–42.

Part 1

Training practices

2

Different approaches to learning and teaching

Introduction

This is an important chapter, as it introduces underpinning approaches to learning and teaching which are relevant in different training situations. If a trainer has a basic understanding of these approaches then s/he will be able to ensure that their training activities are logical, coherent and designed to meet the needs of diverse participants.

This chapter focuses on the following themes:

- three approaches to learning and teaching
- a model for workplace learning programmes
- theories of learning.

The chapter starts by exploring three different approaches: content or trainer-centred approaches, where the focus is on what is to be taught; learner-centred approaches, which, as the name implies, put learners at the centre of the learning process; and social approaches to learning. There is overlap between learner-centred and social approaches to learning. Social approaches to learning are very relevant to trainers, as – particularly in continuous professional development – learning communities are often developed as part of the training strategy. In reality, an individual's training practice rarely fits so neatly into any one of these three categories, but may involve a blend of content- or trainer-centred approaches, learner-centred approaches and social approaches.

In recent years there has been a shift in emphasis from traditional face-to-face training sessions and towards designing development programmes which are integrated into workplace practices. This is called the 70:20:10 model and it is explored in this chapter. This model is very relevant to library and information trainers who are developing training programmes in which training events are integrated into workplace learning activities (explored in Chapter 8).

Finally, the chapter ends with an exploration of three learning theories. The section starts by looking at three different models of learning style (VAK, Honey and Mumford, Dunn and Dunn) and their relevance to training. This is followed by two models of learning: Bloom's Taxonomy of Learning; and the Learning Competences model. The Bloom's Taxonomy of Learning model provides an insight into the design of learning outcomes, and also of learning activities, and into the need for these to be aligned. The Learning Competence model is relevant both to the design of training events and to people's behaviours as they learn something new.

It is worth noting that there is an extensive theoretical literature on learning and teaching. The content of this chapter is very much a summary and synthesis of these ideas. Further information can be found in books and other materials identified in the list of 'References and additional resources'.

Three approaches to learning and teaching
Content or trainer-centred approach

The content- or trainer-centred approach, as its name suggests, places the content of the course delivered by the trainer at the centre of the learning process. In this approach to training, the trainer is considered to be an expert who transfers his or her knowledge or skills, via presentations and structured activities, to the learners or participants, whose job is to learn everything that is presented to them. This means that the learner's role is rather passive – a little like a container waiting to be filled. This is sometimes called 'the sage on the stage' approach to training, and it is a transmission process based on the idea that learning involves 'filling up' the learner with knowledge.

Typical examples of content- or trainer-centred learning and teaching activities include didactic lectures or presentations, and also traditional computer-aided learning packages that are based on the idea of 'drill and practice'. These include web-based training programmes that transmit chunks of knowledge to the learner and then use question-and-answer techniques or activities to reinforce the learning.

One common feature of this approach to learning is that the learners have little choice about what they will learn. Tutor-centred approaches are sometimes linked to an underlying theory of teaching and learning called behaviourism, in which learning activities and processes are clearly labelled, observed and measured. These are typified by:

- very specific definition of learning objectives
- material broken down into small chunks and linked in a clear, logical sequence
- emphasis on knowledge and skill reproduction
- learning activities sequenced by the trainer
- frequent tests or reviews that test the ability to reproduce key facts or ideas
- little awareness of or allowance for individuals' perspectives or experiences.

This approach to teaching and learning is relevant in certain types of situation where individuals are required to learn specific information, e.g. definitions of terms, standard referencing techniques. However, it is less relevant to situations where the subject is constantly changing and individuals need to deal with complex situations or conflicting datasets or information. This approach to training is often used when the trainer wants to describe a particular service or resource, e.g. the library service or a particular e-resource; or give guidance on searching a particular topic. It is also commonly used when there is a lack of time. This is demonstrated in the following example and case study.

Example 2.1 Library induction

Anju is a library tutor in a sixth form college. Each year she has the opportunity to speak to new students as part of their induction programme. She is very aware that she is one of many people who lecture to them in their first few days. Her lecture is brief, and in it she puts across the following messages:

- Her job is to help learners to do well on their courses and get good results.
- The library contains lots of different resources: books, magazines, newspapers, e-resources.
- The students will have to spend time learning how to use the library. This will help them to obtain up-to-date resources and will be a useful skill if they go on to further or higher education.

This is a didactic session and there is no interaction in it. However, the session is followed up later in the term by interactive and very learner-centred workshops in the library.

Case study 2.1 Working in a government research centre

Janet is an information scientist working in a specialist government research centre. The staff in the research centre have a monthly research-project briefing meeting which normally lasts two hours. Janet obtained permission from the research director to speak for up to 10 minutes at each of these meetings. She uses this time to update the staff on new resources or specialist search features relevant to the current projects. Each session follows the same format: using PowerPoint she demonstrates the resource or search technique, and she uses screen grabs to demonstrate the different facilities. She uploads these PowerPoint presentations to the research centre's intranet after each meeting. Overall, the sessions are well received and Janet says that the research director would have cancelled them if she didn't think they were effective or a good use of the researchers' time.

TIP FOR TRAINERS
If you expect your participants to learn specific information, then think about different and interesting ways of putting it across to them. Examples include quizzes, participant presentations, workbooks, case studies (see later in this book).

Learner-centred approaches

Learner-centred approaches to teaching and learning are concerned with enabling individuals to participate in active and relevant learning experiences. There are three characteristics of learner-centred learning:

- The learner is actively involved in the learning process.
- Learning is based on real-life and authentic situations.
- Learning is treated as a social process.

This approach is linked to the concept of deep and surface approaches to learning (e.g. see Entwistle, 1981). Individuals who adopt a deep approach to learning are concerned with the meaning of what they are studying and the ways in which an idea will fit into existing knowledge structures. Consequently, they develop a much deeper and more complex understanding of their subject. In contrast, individuals who adopt a surface approach to learning are concerned with remembering the topic, e.g. for an examination, and so have a limited grasp of the subject. The implication for learners is that by becoming actively involved in the subject and working towards understanding the meaning of the ideas that they are studying, they are more likely to develop a deep understanding of the subject. This idea is developed in the section later in this chapter on Bloom's Taxonomy of Learning.

In learner-centred approaches to training the events are likely to begin by identifying the learners' starting position, e.g. their current knowledge and skills, and then identifying their desired goals and outcomes. This often involves a negotiation process. In learner-centred learning, training activities are likely to be based on real-life and authentic situations that are relevant to the individual learners. This process may involve participants in discussions about their starting-points and learning requirements, and it may mean that they identify how they will achieve their learning goals. Consequently, learning becomes a negotiated process that involves dialogue between the learners and trainers. In the learner-centred model, individuals learn as a result of interactions with others and their learning is dependent on themselves and their interactions with others, both peers and trainers.

Example 2.2 Carrying out a literature search

Alper runs a regular workshop for PhD learners in the field of education, to help them carry out their literature review. He uses a learner-centred approach, and a typical workshop involves students working in groups and exploring the following topics:

1 importance of the literature review
2 characteristics of good quality literature reviews (exercise based on completed PhD theses)
3 key databases in their discipline (education)
4 searching for their topic

5   advanced search techniques.

Alper does not lecture to the students but gets them to work in groups based on their areas of research. He provides them with printed guides and handouts to reinforce the session. Afterwards, he offers them one-to-one sessions where he will help them with their specific research topics.

Learning as a social activity

Learner-centred or student-centred approaches to learning are often linked to the idea that learning is a social process. This means that it is important for trainers to provide participants with opportunities for working in pairs or groups and to provide time for discussions and interactions both within the training event and also during breaks.

A development of this idea is the concept of a learning community, and this is often described using the metaphor of a 'community of practice'. Wenger et al. (2002) have defined the phrase 'communities of practice' as:

> groups of people who share a concern, a set of problems, or a passion about a topic, and who deepen their knowledge and expertise in this area by interacting on an ongoing basis.
>
> (Wenger et al., 2002, 4)

The work of Wenger and his colleagues is based on the assumption that learners are social beings, that individuals learn when they make connections between ideas and their experiences and that knowledge may be developed by working with others in shared enterprises. Translating this into practice, this means that one approach to supporting individual development is to set up learning groups or communities. These can be free flowing and develop out of existing communities of interest and networks, and social networking tools such as LinkedIn are particularly helpful here. Alternatively, they may be managed or facilitated, and this means that facilitators or trainers enable the community to work towards goals that match those of the organization.

Being a member of a learning community or community of practice brings a range of potential benefits, as listed below:

- workplace benefits, including:
  — access to information and expertise
  — wider perspective on problems and issues
  — opportunities for sharing resources
  — opportunity to find innovative solutions to complex problems
- social benefits, including:
  — access to like-minded individuals

— support and friendship
— sense of identity and group membership
— opportunity to 'let off steam' in a safe environment
- career benefits, including:
— confidence building
— development of professional expertise
— continuing professional development
— professional networking.

(Adapted from Lewis and Allan, 2005)

Examples of communities of practice in library and information work include: professional bodies and their specialist groups; project groups; special interest groups; some user groups. Chapter 7 provides examples of online learning communities. These are often used as a means of promoting professional development within the library and information professions. Evaluations of communities of practice demonstrate that they are particularly helpful for three groups (Lewis and Allan, 2005):

- new entrants to a profession; communities of practice can provide newly qualified professionals with ready access to established practitioners' knowledge and experience as well as experienced role models
- individuals who are moving into situations that are new to them, e.g. as a result of a change in employment, in which they want to quickly develop relevant knowledge and expertise
- individuals who are working at the forefront of specialist knowledge and tackling new problems and unique situations; communities of practice provide them with access to experienced colleagues with whom they can discuss and construct knowledge and develop new approaches to practice.

Many communities of practice operate through face-to-face meetings, e-mails and group discussions online. They may be established by trainers as a means of enabling a group to focus on a particular challenge or problem, e.g. the introduction of a new system or service. In contrast, some communities develop spontaneously, e.g. through social networking sites such as LinkedIn.

Case study 2.2 Training-the-trainer community of practice
The author led a train-the-trainer two-day event for librarians from a number of European countries. The event went well, and during the final afternoon delegates discussed keeping in touch with each other. Consequently, they set up a closed Google Group and used this to share ideas, training materials and experiences. The group was lively for about 15 months and then fizzled out.

During its lively phase, three group members were extremely active participants in the group. According to Wenger et al. (2002) they were core members, while other members were 'peripheral participants', as they were on the fringes of the group but still logged in at regular intervals and contributed to discussions every so often. The change in employment of two of the core members meant that they stopped participating regularly in the group, and this led to its coming to a natural end.

TIP FOR TRAINERS

Have you built in opportunities for your course participants to socialize? This can take place through:

- tea or coffee breaks
- activities involving discussions, e.g. pair, trio or small-group activities
- small-group tasks, e.g. developing a presentation, producing something on a whiteboard or flipchart, or completing quizzes or questionnaires in pairs or trios.

Many people find that these types of activities give them an opportunity to network and also to talk about their own concerns, issues or thoughts about the topics covered in the training course.

A model for workplace learning programmes

The 70:20:10 model of workplace learning and training was developed by staff at the Centre for Creative Leadership (2011) and the basic idea is that successful learning and development in the workplace involves:

- 70% on-the-job learning experiences
- 20% social learning
- 10% learning from courses and reading.

The model is essentially a prescriptive one and it was developed in the context of management and leadership development.

The 70% on-the-job learning experiences are concerned with 'learning by doing', which also ensures that the learning is embedded in the reality of day-to-day life at work (see Chapter 8). This may include:

- taking on new specific tasks, work experience, projects, problem solving
- horizontal moves within the library or information service
- covering for an absent colleague
- job rotation
- promotion
- action learning (see Chapter 3).

The 20% which relates to social aspects of learning may include:

- learning from feedback
- asking for help and advice
- shadowing an experienced colleague
- mentoring or networking.

The final 10% of learning from courses is sometimes called 'the amplifier effect', as formal training helps to structure and support on-the-job learning.

Example 2.3 Project management training

Hilary, an independent library trainer, was asked to run a project management training course for a group of information consultants working in the publishing industry. After spending some time with the information consultants' manager to identify the aims and objectives of the course, she produced the programme outline presented in Figure 2.1.

It is worth noting that the breakdown of the time in this development programme doesn't fall neatly into the 70:20:10 rule, but this reflects the reality of the programme. In addition, the time spent in the actual workshops (activities 1, 5 and 8) has been categorized into the 20% field, i.e. social learning. This is because these workshops were developed with an underpinning pedagogy of social theories of learning and involved experiential activities, discussion and reflection.

Theories of learning
Learning styles
Learning is a complex and messy business, and it is difficult to summarize learning theories without the risk of over-simplifying the topic. There are an extremely large number of theories and models of learning styles. The basic idea behind learning styles is that each person has a preferred way of learning new topics or skills. However, this isn't fixed and is dependent on the focus of learning and the context, i.e. the learning environment, and it changes over time.

Three learning style models are considered here: the VAK (visual, auditory, kinaesthetic) model is widely used in schools and colleges; the Honey and Mumford (1992) model has been selected because it is widely used in higher education and in management education; and the Dunn and Dunn (1999) model is included because it provides a very broad perspective on individual approaches to teaching and learning. There are extensive academic debates about the reliability and validity of different models of learning styles. In the context of this book, learning styles are used as a framework for thinking about individual learning preferences and the need to design training sessions to meet these needs.

VAK model
The VAK model of learning comes from a body of knowledge known as neuro-linguistic programming (see, e.g. O'Connor, and Seymour, 1993) and it identifies three basic learning styles:

Course title: Project management for information consultants				
Aim: The purpose of this programme is to enable information consultants to deliver workplace projects on time and within budget				
Learning outcomes: As a result of completing this programme, information consultants will be able to: • use standard project management tools and techniques in the workplace • develop a project proposal and plan using standard project management tools and techniques • deliver a project on time and within budget • manage the project communication processes • reflect on and learn from their own practical project experiences.				
Learning process	**Time scale**	**70%**	**20%**	**10%**
1 Introduction to programme and to project management; basic tools and techniques	1-day workshop (6 hours)		6	
2 Independent study activities: reading specific sections of a guide to project management and watching two videos	12 hours			12
3 Working in pairs, each pair produces a project proposal, shares it online and obtains feedback from the trainer, their manager and the rest of the group	20-day period (equivalent to 30 hours' work on programme)	30		
4 Continuing to work in the same pair, each pair produces a project plan, shares it online and obtains feedback from the trainer and the rest of the group	20-day period (equivalent to 20 hours' work on programme)	20		
5 Trainer-led workshop on project implementation	Half-day workshop (3 hours)		3	
6 Independent study activities: reading specific sections of a guide to project management and watching a video	8 hours			8
7 Pairs implement their project and receive feedback from their manager on a weekly basis plus coaching sessions with their trainer	20-day period (equivalent to 24 hours' work on the programme) 4 x 1 hour's feedback from manager 2 x 1 hour's coaching sessions from trainer	24	6	
8 Final project workshop involving a presentation, feedback and review session involving whole group, manager and trainer	Workshop (4 hours)		4	
	Total time spent on different types of activity (hours)	74	19	20

Figure 2.1 *Project management training using the 70:20:10 approach*

• visual, i.e. involving seeing, reading, diagrams, pictures
• auditory, i.e. involving listening and speaking
• kinaesthetic, i.e. involving touching, doing and feeling.

There are many free self-assessment questionnaires available on the VAK model[1] and they are fun to complete as a tool to encourage reflection on approaches to learning. In terms of training sessions, this model provides a reminder that it is important to use all the senses in the course of a training event.

Honey and Mumford model

The Honey and Mumford (1992) model is based on the ideas of Kolb (1984) and it is now widely used in both academic and commercial learning and teaching situations. Peter Honey and Alan Mumford identified four main learning styles (activist, pragmatist, reflector, theorist – see Table 2.1) and suggested that individuals may work around a learning cycle (see Figure 2.2). They produced tools for identifying individual learning styles and these are available online.[2]

The Honey and Mumford model offers an over-simplification of the learning process, e.g. Figure 2.2 suggests that learners move around a cyclical process in a linear manner. My own experience is that learning is a more complex process than is implied by the model; learners may move around the cycle in different ways and spend varying amounts of time at each stage. In addition, individual learners may be involved in a number of processes at the same time, e.g. my own style of reflection is through activities such as writing or talking. Despite these limitations, the model does have the benefit of providing a simple framework that learners can use to explore and reflect on their own experiences. However, it must be emphasized that this model and the results of using self-assessment tools such as learning-styles questionnaires should not be used to stereotype individuals or groups.

Dunn and Dunn model

The Dunn and Dunn (1999) model of learning styles was developed by researchers in the USA who identified seven aspects of learning: perceptual; information processing; problem solving; environmental; physiological; emotional; and sociological. Each of these aspects is then divided into a series of preferred learning styles, which are listed in Table 2.2. It is possible to use this model of learning styles to identify individual preferences by completing the third column in Table 2.2 or by using online tools available at sites such as www. learningstyles.net.

These three models of learning styles are relevant to trainers, as they provide insights into individual learning preferences. They may be used in a number of different ways:

1 Learning-styles questionnaires may be used by individual learners or trainers to identify and reflect on their own learning preferences.
2 The VAK model may be used to check that all the senses are engaged during the training event.
3 The Honey and Mumford model provides guidance on designing training or coaching sessions. Each of the learning styles covers a stage in the training session, and this is sometimes called the 4MAT method. This is explored in

Table 2.1 Honey and Mumford four learning styles	
Learning style	**Approach to learning**
Pragmatist	Pragmatists take a practical approach to their studies. They want to know that what they are studying is relevant and useful to either their assessed work and/or the workplace. They enjoy practical tasks and activities such as case studies and problem-based learning. They don't enjoy abstract theories, particularly if they can't see their relevance to everyday life. Pragmatists prefer action rather than long-winded discussions and they want to 'get on with the job'. They often ask questions about the relationships between what they are studying and 'real life'.
Activist	Activists will often dive into situations and 'get on with it'. They enjoy learning through activities, case studies or work-based learning and they can quickly become bored if there is too much discussion or theory. Activists tend to enjoy practical activities and opportunities to do something creative or different. They are less keen on detailed research and planning activities, and they may become bored rather quickly. Many activists don't like to work by themselves, as they prefer to be part of a group and enjoy the social side of learning.
Reflector	Reflectors like time and space to think things through carefully before coming to a conclusion. They are most comfortable when they have access to all the relevant information, and time to make a considered decision. Reflectors are very good at working through a problem or set of ideas and they will often identify issues that other people have not noticed. They sometimes find it hard to keep to deadlines, as they need to consider all the relevant information and every possibility. In addition, they may become frustrated if asked to complete activities over a very short time span, as this doesn't provide them with sufficient time to think or reflect on the subject. Some reflectors appear to be quiet or shy; however, this is because they are thinking deeply about the topic. Reflectors are often extremely uncomfortable if they are put on the spot and asked to voice their opinion. They need time to think and to reflect on the topic.
Theorist	Theorists like to know the reasons behind things and they have a methodical and logical approach to their subject. They like to analyse ideas in a logical way and they will ask questions and make mental connections until they have integrated new ideas or theories into their existing knowledge. They are not usually happy with subjective judgements or with making decisions on the basis of scant evidence. Theorists are often perfectionists with set ways of doing things and this can mean that they find it frustrating if they are dealing with contradictory information. They pay attention to detail, and this is a great strength, but it can also slow them down and prevent them from completing their work on time.

Figure 2.2 Honey and Mumford learning styles model

Table 2.2 *Dunn and Dunn model of learning styles*		
Learning style aspects	Learning style preferences	List your own preferences using the different items listed under 'Learning style preferences'
Perceptual	Auditory Visual – picture Visual – text Tactile and/or kinaesthetic Verbal kinaesthetic	
Processing	Analytical – step by step Global – metaphor, 'big picture' Integrated – analytical plus global	
Problem solving	Reflective Impulsive	
Environmental	Sound Light Temperature Seating	
Physiological	Time of day Intake Mobility	
Emotional	Motivation Persistence Conformity Structure	
Sociological	Team Authority Variety	

greater detail in Chapter 5.

4 Learning style preferences, e.g. the Dunn and Dunn list in Table 2.2, may be used to reflect on the design of a training programme – how are the different learning style preferences covered in the design? The relevance of this model to training is that it provides a framework for designing training events (see Chapter 5).

TIP FOR TRAINERS

There is an impressive research base on the subject of learning styles. Be careful about how you approach this topic. If you are spending a relatively short amount of time on it, then you need to frame your work to highlight that, in the time available, you are providing a generalized and over-simplified approach to the subject.

I find it useful to remind participants that: concepts of learning styles are useful as a means of reflecting on approaches to learning; we are all very sophisticated and flexible – our learning styles are unlikely to be fixed, and indeed they change over time and context. Finally, it is important not to use them to stereotype or label ourselves or others.

Bloom's Taxonomy of Learning

How do trainers decide on the focus of their training events? How do they help to ensure that the training is at the appropriate level? What are the right words to describe the type of learning that is intended in training events? Bloom's (1956) Taxonomy of Learning provides a framework for understanding the different levels of learning achieved within a training session. The outline presented here is a simplified overview and some of Bloom's original language has been changed to make it more accessible. There are six levels relating to learning new knowledge:

1 Remembering
2 Understanding
3 Application
4 Analysis
5 Evaluation
6 Creation.

Each of these levels may be linked to particular learning achievements, and so may be used to develop learning outcomes and assessment activities. For example, Level 1, Remembering is concerned with being able to remember, list, define, describe. A full breakdown of Bloom's taxonomy and its links to verbs which may be used to develop learning outcomes or prepare assessment activities is presented in Table 2.3. This table also indicates the shift from surface to deep learning that takes place during movement from Levels 1 to 6.

Table 2.3 *Bloom's Taxonomy of Learning (Adapted from Anderson and Krathwohl, 2001)*

Levels of cognition	Learner is able to	Deep or surface learning
1 Remembering	Remember, list, define, describe	Surface
2 Understanding	Explain, summarize, rephrase	
3 Application	Use in new or different situations, implement	
4 Analysis	Compare, organize, deconstruct	
5 Evaluation	Judge, set and use criteria to evaluate, prioritize	
6 Creation	Design, build, construct, produce	Deep

How is this relevant to training? Bloom's taxonomy provides a structure for deciding the level of learning that you want to achieve within a training session. This is illustrated in Table 2.4. All levels are important, and this taxonomy provides helpful guidance for planning training sessions and ensuring that the activities are designed and delivered at an appropriate level, as illustrated in the final column of Table 2.4. These ideas are applied in practice in Chapter 5, where the focus is on the design of training events.

Table 2.4 *Bloom's taxonomy of learning – application in practice (Adapted from Anderson and Krathwohl, 2001)*

Levels of cognition	Learner is able to	Example application	Example learning activities
Remembering	Remember, list, define, describe	Describe the layout of the library	Tour Treasure hunt
Understanding	Explain, summarize, rephrase	Explain why referencing is important for lawyers	Lecture Podcast Study guide
Application	Use in new or different situations, implement	Use Boolean logic in a different online search	Demonstration Hands-on session
Analysis	Compare, organize, deconstruct	Compare and contrast two information sources	Practical exercise Discussion Producing a report
Evaluation	Judge, set and use criteria to evaluate, prioritize	Evaluate the relevance of a learning resource for a particular group of learners	Practical activity Discussion Reflection
Creation	Design, build, construct, produce	Write an evidence-based literature review	Independent learning, e.g. project work

Levels of competence

The final learning model explored in this chapter is the levels of competence (illustrated in Figure 2.3), which is concerned with one's ability to know and be able to do something (a more detailed explanation is available at Business Balls, 2012). There are four stages in this model:

- unconscious incompetence – 'I don't know what I don't know'
- conscious incompetence – 'I know that I don't know it'
- conscious competence – 'I know how to do something and it involves effort'
- unconscious competence – 'I know how to do this and I can do it without much effort'.

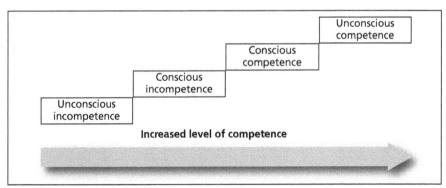

Figure 2.3 *Competence model*

How is this relevant to trainers? Someone who is not reading this book may be in a state of unconscious incompetence (I don't know what I don't know) regarding a particular training concept, for example Bloom's Taxonomy of Learning. However, someone who picks up the book and reads this section may be in a state of conscious incompetence (I know that I don't know it). Such a person may then decide to apply this model to the design of their next training session, and this will involve effort. They may need to keep checking back with the model and asking colleagues for help. This is the stage of conscious competence (I know how to do something and it involves effort). After using Bloom's taxonomy to help them design numerous training sessions, they are likely to find that they can use it without any effort, i.e. they are in a state of unconscious competence (I know how to do this and I can do it without much effort).

This model is also relevant to people's behaviour on training courses, as shown in the following examples:

- Jane, a liaison librarian in a university, uses a challenging diagnostic quiz with first-year learners to help them to understand that they need to 'go beyond Google' if they are to be successful in an academic environment. The diagnostic quiz is designed to make a grade of more than 50% very hard to achieve, i.e. it helps to shift the learners from unconscious incompetence to conscious incompetence.
- Prudence, an independent trainer, runs open training sessions. She finds that her participants arrive very highly motivated and keen to learn, i.e. they are in a state of either conscious incompetence or conscious competence. She is able to harness this energy and enthusiasm.
- Mark, a knowledge management trainer in a company, frequently trains people who have been 'sent on his courses' by their manager. He finds that these people may be in a state of unconscious incompetence (in which case a diagnostic exercise helps them to see that they can benefit from the course) or they may be in a state of unconscious competence, in which case he helps them to learn additional facets about their systems. He always takes 'advanced' exercises with him for these types of people. Mark also finds that there are one or two people who come on his courses with attitude problems that have nothing to do with their level of competence. He uses his interpersonal skills to deal with them.
- Agata was leading the training for library staff in using a new self-service system. One of the members of staff was having great difficulty in using the system and kept talking about 'the good old days of the previous desk services'. Agata realized from observation that this person could actually use the system but was distracting herself (and others) with her comments. She decided to give her lots of practice, and so to help this colleague to move from a state of conscious competence to one of unconscious competence.

Summary

There are a number of different general approaches to learning and teaching, and these have been described in this chapter as:

- content or tutor centred
- learner centred
- social approaches to learning.

In addition, the 70:20:10 workplace model for learning and development has been introduced here. This model emphasizes the importance of workplace learning activities, and these are considered in some detail in Chapter 8.

Finally, three learning theories have been explored in this chapter:

- models of learning styles:
  — VAK
  — Honey and Mumford
  — Dunn and Dunn
- Bloom's Taxonomy of Learning
- the competence learning model.

In reality, individual trainers may use a combination of approaches to learning and teaching in their practice, as is demonstrated in the following case study.

Example 2.4 Different approaches to learning and teaching

Federica, a trainer in a large public library, describes her approaches to learning and teaching as follows:

I use a combination of methods. Sometimes, I am very didactic, e.g. I use detailed PowerPoint presentations and worksheets to take staff through what they need to learn so as to be able to use our different IT systems. It is definitely me in control and leading what everyone learns. Otherwise, we wouldn't achieve the learning objectives. I have a chart of Bloom's taxonomy in my office and this helps me to get the language right.

I run some sessions for teenagers to help them to use online resources for their GCSE or A level studies. Here I am much more learner focused. We use the VAK model – lots of schools around here use it. I make sure that I have a variety of exercises and activities to cover all three learning styles in the session. I ask them to choose their own topic and then help them to evaluate different information sources using checklists and guides. They help each other during these sessions and there is normally a lot of chat and laughter. [Laughs] From the outside, it probably looks chaotic and people wouldn't think there was a trainer in the room. It works, and they recommend the sessions to their friends.

Finally, my staff development sessions are often more about sharing experience and practice, e.g. I run a session on dealing with challenging readers and most of the time we share horror stories and how we dealt with the individuals. The only didactic bit in these sessions is when I present the local authority's various policies that we must follow in these situations.

Notes

1 Two examples are www.businessballs.com/vaklearningstylestest.htm and www.brainboxx.co.uk/a3_aspects/pages/VAK.htm.
2 Examples include www.peterhoney.com and www.brainboxx.co.uk/a2_learningstyles.

References and additional resources

Anderson, L. W. and Krathwohl, D. R. (2001) *A Taxonomy for Learning, Teaching and Assessing: a revision of Bloom's Taxonomy of Educational Objectives*, Pearson Education Group.

Bloom, B. S. (1956) *Taxonomy of Educational Objectives, Handbook 1: the cognitive domain*, David McKay Co. Inc.

Boud, D., Keogh, R. and Walker, D. (1985) *Reflection: turning experience into learning*, Croom Helm.

Business Balls (2012) *Conscious Competence Learning Model*, www.businessballs.com/consciouscompetencelearningmodel.htm [accessed on 12 August 2012].

Centre for Creative Leadership (2011) The 70:20:10 Rule, *Leading Effectively E-newsletter*, www.ccl.org/leadership/enewsletter/2011/NOVrule.aspx [Accessed on 27 January 2012].

Dunn, R. and Dunn, K. (1999) *The Complete Guide to the Learning Styles Inservice System*, Allyn & Bacon.

Entwistle, N. (1981) *Styles of Learning and Teaching: an integrated outline of educational psychology for students, teachers and lecturers*, John Wiley.

Honey, P. and Mumford, A. (1992) *Manual of Learning Styles*, Peter Honey Publishing.

Kolb, D. A. (1984) *Experiential Learning: experience as the source of learning and development*, Prentice-Hall.

Laurillard, D. (2002) *Rethinking University Teaching: a framework for the effective use of educational technology*, 2nd edn, Routledge Falmer.

Lave, J. and Wenger, E. (1991) *Situated Learning: legitimate peripheral participation*, Cambridge University Press.

Lewis, D. and Allan, B. (2005) *Virtual Learning Communities*, Open University Press.

O'Connor, J. and Seymour, J. (1993) *Introducing NLP: neuro-linguistic programming*, HarperCollins.

Wenger, E. (1998) *Communities of Practice: learning, meaning and identity*, Cambridge University Press.

Wenger, E., McDermott, R. and Snyder, W. (2002) *Cultivating Communities of Practice: a guide to managing knowledge*, Harvard Business School Press.

3

Making training interesting

Introduction

The purpose of this chapter is to provide an overview of different methods of delivering learning and teaching. A combination of these different methods may be included in a training session in order to engage the learners and enhance their learning experience. The training methods are listed in alphabetical order.

Additional training methods which involve the use of ICTs are described in Chapter 4, and Chapter 8 provides a guide to over 90 workplace learning activities which may be incorporated into training programmes.

Action planning

Action plans are frequently used as a means of encouraging learners to identify what they are going to do either during or after the training event. The process of writing an action plan and then sharing it with peers, trainers or work colleagues can be extremely motivating. The key to a good action plan is that it should be SMART:

- Specific, i.e. the action is identifiable
- Measurable, i.e. there is something to see or hear that will show that the action has taken place
- Achievable, i.e. the action is manageable within the context of the training course and the working environment of the library
- Relevant, i.e. the learner will immediately understand its relevance to him or her
- Time bound, i.e. a deadline is set for the action, or time is allocated to it on a regular basis.

A simple and practical approach to action planning is to hand out a sticky note to each participant and ask her/him to identify and write down an action that they will do as a result of the training event. They can then share this with a colleague or the whole group. Participants can take the sticky note away with them from the training as a reminder of their intended action. Alternatively, participants can be asked to complete an action planning form – an example is provided in Figure 3.1.

What are you going to do as a result of the workshop?
1 What do you want to do? Choose a particular task or activity.
2 When will you do it?
3 Where will you do it?
4 Will you be working by yourself or with someone else? If you are working with someone else, then have you obtained his or her agreement?
5 Is there anything that will stop you from doing it? How can you prevent this from happening?
6 What will be the benefit (to you or your library) of completing this action?

Figure 3.1 *Example form used for action planning*

Activities

Most trainers develop a range of activities which help them to engage learners in the topic under consideration. A general principle for all activities is that you need to:

- identify a clear learning outcome for the activity
- require an output from the activity, either by individuals or by groups
- think about the levels of experience and confidence of participants
- think about how you will support individuals who have additional needs
- think about how you will allocate people to groups (or let them choose for themselves) and the size of the groups, if you want them to work in groups
- think about how you will start and end the activity.

Advantages of activities:

- The learners have an opportunity to 'learn from doing'.
- Individuals can apply their own experience to the activity.
- They provide an opportunity for people to learn in groups.
- It is possible to provide a range of activities, e.g. of varying difficulty, to meet the needs of people of different abilities.
- They can be used to change the pace of the training session.
- They give the trainer a 'rest' from leading the group from the front.

Disadvantages of activities:

- They can be time consuming.
- Individuals don't always learn what is expected from the activity.
- Individuals may go 'off task' and use the time for catching up on news or e-mails.

Chapter 4 provides examples of the use of technology in developing activities for training events.

Examples of these activities include:

- case studies
- discussion groups
- games
- hands-on sessions
- ice-breakers
- surveys and questionnaires
- treasure hunts.

Case studies

A case study is an example based on a real-life situation. For example, this book provides many case studies, which are used to demonstrate how trainers, working in the context of library and information services, design or deliver training. Some of these case studies demonstrate the variance between theory and practice.

Participants in a training programme may be given a case study which will typically include the following information:

- description of a real-life situation
- necessary background information, facts and figures
- supporting materials
- questions to consider.

However, as is demonstrated by the case study presented in this section, they may be very brief. While working on a case study, participants may be asked to:

- identify key issues
- suggest the best solution(s)
- reflect on their learning.

Advantages of case studies include:

- Participants can learn from discussing a real-life situation.
- They encourage peer learning.
- They can be very engaging.

Disadvantages include:

- They take time to prepare and pilot.
- The case study may be an over-simplification.
- It may be set in a context different from that of the participants, who may then find it difficult to engage with the case study.

Example 3.1 Teaching large groups

I use the following very short case study in a training session for librarians on teaching large groups. The exercise and reporting take about 10 minutes. The exercise is presented on a PowerPoint slide and I ask participants to work in groups of three or four.

Case study: Teaching large groups

- You are asked to present a 50-minute lecture to 300 first-year students. You are advised that there are a number of students with special needs in the group: two students are dyslexic; one has a visual impairment and one a hearing impairment.

- How will you take these students into account in the design and delivery of your lecture?

Demonstrations

Demonstrations are commonly used as a means of providing individuals or groups with an overview of a particular system or database. This may involve a PowerPoint presentation or a 'live' demonstration. For live demonstrations it can be helpful if one person talks through the demonstration while another works the technology. A number of computer-based tools are available to help produce good-quality demonstrations, and these are outlined in Chapter 4.

Trainers need to take care to:

- plan the demonstration carefully
- link the demonstration to the interests of the audience
- keep it simple
- provide supporting materials, e.g. handouts
- provide a summary
- provide participants with the opportunity to practise for themselves
- have a contingency plan.

Advantages of demonstrations are that they:

- provide a means of demonstrating something to a large group
- provide an opportunity for pointing out key features or facilities.

Disadvantages of demonstrations are that:

- the pace may be too slow/quick for some individuals
- the participants may feel overwhelmed by the skill of the trainer and think that they will never achieve the same level of competence
- the demonstration may go wrong, or there may be technical problems.

Example 3.2 Demonstrations in an academic context

Laura, an academic liaison librarian, uses demonstrations to teach students how to use databases. She made the following comments about her practice:

I normally e-mail either the students (if they are a small group) or their lecturer (if it is a large group) and ask them about possible search topics. If the students have an assignment coming up, then I will use that topic. I e-mail them in advance and this encourages attendance. I like to do live searches, but always have alternative slides within my PowerPoint presentation (this involves using the hyperlink function) just in case there are problems using the database or it is very slow. It also means that when I post the slides up on Blackboard (the virtual learning system) students can look at the whole presentation. I find it hard to speak to the group, type in a live search and also keep control. So, whenever possible I ask a colleague to help me out by doing the typing. If this isn't possible, then I ask for a student volunteer – normally this works, but I've found it best to give them a sheet with the search terms printed on it – I don't want to embarrass anyone whose spelling is weak. This works, but it takes a lot of preparation. Finally, I keep demonstrations short. Up to five minutes is long enough. If you go any longer, then you can see people switching off. I often do five minutes' talk, five minutes' demo, and then keep going like that until the end.

Case study 3.1 Teaching Boolean logic

Deborah, a liaison librarian in a university college, teaches basic search techniques to large groups of students in lecture theatres. She has developed an exercise for teaching Boolean logic that is based on what people had for breakfast. It involves different groups standing up and then demonstrating AND, OR and NOT logic as follows:

Introduction to the activity

What did you have for breakfast? Deborah starts by explaining the reason for the exercise and asking any students who didn't have coffee, toast or cereal for breakfast to act as observers and report back to the whole group what happened at each stage of the exercise.

Exercise set-up

Deborah asks three different groups of students to identify themselves and stand up:

- Stand up if you had a cup of coffee. Thank you, you may sit down now.
- Stand up if you had cereal. Thank you, you may sit down now.
- Stand up if you had toast. Thank you, you may sit down now.

She reminds the observers to remember roughly how many people stood up each time.

OR logic

- Deborah then asks those people who had **coffee OR cereal** to stand up. She reminds the observers to notice what is happening.
- She then asks people who had **coffee OR cereal OR toast** to stand up. While they are standing up she asks the observers to comment on the difference between the two groups (coffee OR cereal; coffee OR cereal OR toast).

AND logic

- The next stage is to identify AND logic, and this involves Deborah asking all of those who had **coffee OR cereal** to stand up again. She reminds the observers to notice what is happening.
- She then asks those people who had **coffee AND cereal** to remain standing. She thanks

the others and asks them to sit down.
- Deborah then asks the observers to comment on the differences between the OR and the AND groups.

NOT
- In the final stage Deborah asks those people who had **cereal AND toast** to stand up. Again, she reminds the observers to notice what is happening.
- She then asks those people who are standing who did **NOT** have **toast** to sit down.
- She then asks the observers to comment on the impact of the **NOT** command.

Deborah then thanks everyone for their participation in the exercise and asks them to sit down. She then debriefs the exercise using a PowerPoint presentation which summarizes the key features of Boolean logic and the use of the **AND, OR** and **NOT** operators.

Discussion groups
Discussion groups are often used in training sessions, as they are a useful way of enabling:

- individuals to feel relaxed in a training session
- experienced practitioners to share their practice
- less-experienced individuals to discuss specific issues or concerns
- a break from a lecture, demonstration or hands-on practice.

If you are planning a session where you include discussion activities, then it is a good idea to:

- identify a clear focus of discussion and summarize it on a slide or handout
- require an output from the discussion, e.g. a summary on flipchart paper or sticky notes, or verbal feedback to the whole group
- think about how you will divide people into groups, and the size of the groups
- think about how you will start and end the activity.

When you are running a discussion activity it is a good idea to:

- clearly present the learning outcome, the task, the outputs and the timing – summarizing all of these on one PowerPoint slide produces a useful reference tool during the activity
- start the activity in a very clear style
- monitor the activity, e.g. by listening to the volume of discussions
- avoid interfering in the activity; let individuals take responsibility for their learning

- signal the end of the activity, e.g. by announcing 'You have four minutes left for this activity'
- clearly end the activity
- ask for feedback from each group or a selection of the groups
- thank everyone for engaging in the activity.

Example 3.3 Discussion group in a training session on 'Enhancing your presentations'

Abdul ran a two-hour training session on 'Enhancing your presentations'. Following the introduction to the session, he divided the participants into four groups of four librarians each and asked individuals to work with people whom they did not know well. Once the groups were formed, he asked them to identify the qualities of good and poor presentations, and to write these on flipchart paper. He allowed five minutes for the exercise. At the end of the time Abdul asked each group to post its flipchart paper on the wall. The whole group was then asked to stand up and read all the posters. After a few minutes of reading and informal discussion, Abdul indicated the end of the activity and asked everyone to sit down. He then moved on to the next part of the training session.

Drop-in sessions

Drop-in sessions occur when an individual trainer (or even a group of trainers) provides opportunities for their learners to come and see them at a specific time period. Drop-in sessions may take place in the trainer's office, at a help desk or in a training room. One of the challenges of drop-in sessions is that any number of people could turn up for the session, or no one may be there.

Advantages of drop-in sessions:

- They can be focused on the immediate needs of the individual.
- They provide a means of one-to-one instruction.
- They are particularly useful for busy professionals who are unable or unwilling to attend training events.

Disadvantages of drop-in sessions:

- A large number of individuals may arrive at the same time and require different kinds of help.
- Individuals may arrive with unexpected queries or unrealistic expectations.

Techniques for managing drop-in sessions:

- Have prepared information and guidance sheets with you.
- Make sure that you have a strategy for dealing with numbers of people turning up at the same time.

- Bring work with you in case no one attends the session.

Case study 3.2 Supporting research students

Jane worked in a university which had a relatively small group (under 40) of research students. These students were spread across different schools and faculties. Jane organized a one-day course for them on 'Searching the literature' and this was very well received. Feedback from the students indicated that they would welcome a regular opportunity to receive help from Jane. Consequently, she organized weekly drop-in sessions, open to all research students, which took place in an IT room. Each week between 8 and 12 students attended these sessions, sometimes for just a few minutes, but a few students developed the habit of working in the IT room for the whole of the session. The drop-in sessions became an important part of the research students' experience and the students nominated Jane for one of the Student Union's Staff Appreciation Awards.

Games

Smith and Baker (2011) provide a useful literature review of the value of games in library instruction, and although their focus is mainly university students many of their comments are relevant to all library users. They state that games must have the following characteristics:

- They are underpinned by sound pedagogy.
- They reflect real learning needs.
- They establish clear rules.
- They have specific goals that are linked to the learning objectives.

In libraries, a wide range of games have been used including:

- treasure hunts (see later in this chapter) or mystery tours
- game shows (modelled on TV shows)
- quizzes
- board games
- online games.

Games are often used in training sessions as a means of:

- energizing the group
- integrating new ideas
- assessing learning
- promoting teamwork
- fun.

As with any activity, games require time to be spent on designing them, preparing learning materials and testing them, e.g. with friends or colleagues. An important feature of games is that they should be easy to understand and set up, and many trainers use game formats from television or other popular cultures, e.g. pub quizzes. One of the advantages of this approach is that the game players are likely to be familiar with the format and rules, and so require fewer explanations. There are many books available on training games (e.g. Pike and Solem (2000) and Sugar (1998)). Sugar (1998) provides guidance for structuring games (Table 3.1).

Table 3.1 *Structuring game activity*		
Stage	**Time**	**Activity**
Set up	25%	Introduce the game. Set up the groups and layout of the room. Hand out materials. Clarify rules and answer any queries.
Play	50%	Play the game. Start and stop play. Announce winners. Give prize (if appropriate).
Debriefing	25%	Process the game. Link to learning outcomes. Provide time for reflection.

Advantages of games:

- They provide the opportunity for a change of pace and fun.
- They enable teamwork.
- They appeal to some people's learning styles.

Disadvantages of games:

- Some people may think they are a time waster.
- Some people don't like competitions.

Example 3.4 Course design and accreditation game

JISC provides a game, 'Accreditation', as part of its Supporting Responsive Curriculum project. The game was designed to help individuals to learn about the processes involved in course design and accreditation. It is a board game involving two to four players. The board is divided into three sections: strategic approval, detailed planning, final approval.

Further information, including learning resources (game board, cards, rules) is available at: http//wwwjiscdesignstudio.pbworks.com/.

Example 3.5 Student induction and orientation

Smith and Baker (2011) describe the use of two games developed to help to induct and orientate students. The first game, called 'Get a Clue', is a board game with clues placed around the library; the second game, called 'LibraryCraft', is an online game which involves students in using library resources to kill a dragon. The evaluation of the games indicates that students found them entertaining and informative, a good use of their time, and that they helped them to be 'comfortable' in the library environment.

Example 3.6 Learning styles

A card game, called the 'Squiggle Game', which is based on the Honey and Mumford learning styles model (see Chapter 2) is available at: www.brainboxx.co.uk/a2_learnstyles/ pages/Squiggle.htm. It offers a fun approach to learning styles in training sessions, but it is important to be aware of warnings about stereotyping.

Example 3.7 Anagrams

It is now possible to produce anagrams very easily using internet-based tools such as Hot Potato (http://hotpot.uvic.ca/) – see Chapter 4, 'Games'. The following is an example of using anagrams to maintain students' interest in a presentation on referencing. The students were introduced to the activity with a slide containing the following information:

Anagram activity
- Anagrams will appear throughout this presentation. They will be presented in a 'gold' box.
- When you see one, copy it down.
- After this lecture:
  — work out the words or phrases
  — write an explanation of each word
  — hand in by 4pm Friday:
    – answers on a sheet of paper with your name and Student ID
    – post box outside undergraduate office.
- Next week – PRIZE draw for the first five correct responses.

This activity helps to motivate students to read the slides carefully, and asking them to write an explanation means that they have to understand the concepts. Giving them a time by which to complete the activity after the taught session means that students whose first language isn't English, and also students with special needs, such as dyslexia, have time to work on the activity. Finally, the prize of a book token acts as a great motivator to complete the activity!

The actual anagrams were:

- slamapigris
- rappashare
- nitquatoo
- sceefrener
- action
- a flea grits him spit
- fence winer grins.

Group work

Group activities can be used as a means of:

- relaxing people at the start of a training course (often called ice-breakers – see later in this chapter)
- enabling people to work together and learn from each other
- managing a large number of people, feedback and debriefing sessions
- giving the trainer a break from presentations or other activities where he/she is the focus of attention.

As with any other learning activity, group work needs a clear learning outcome, a clear description of the activity, a time-frame and also a clear output or product. If the trainer doesn't provide these, then the groups may make up their own tasks or waste time by discussing matters not related to the training session. Stating a clear output or product is important, as this will help to focus the group. Examples of outputs include: a list of key points such as advantages and disadvantages; a completed flipchart paper outlining the topic; being prepared to report back to the whole group.

Example activities for groups include:

- identifying the advantages and disadvantages of a tool, service or other topic
- discussing and prioritizing a series of topics or actions
- deciding on a particular course of action
- producing a visual image, e.g. a mind map or spider diagram
- producing a handout, guide or display
- planning an event or activity
- completing an exercise
- completing a case study
- writing a press release.

Approaches to dividing people into groups:

- Let individuals choose for themselves.
- Allocate everyone a number or letter (1, 2, 3, 4 or A, B, C, D etc.) and ask everyone with the same number or letter to work together in the same group.
- Ask people to work with people they don't know/don't regularly work with.

Example outputs for group work:

- oral report back to the whole group
- written report back, e.g. on flipcharts or whiteboards

- a PowerPoint presentation (or single slide)
- handout or guide
- poster.

Sometimes it is possible to arrange for small groups to give their report to another group and then for this to be cascaded around the whole group. For example, two people report to another pair, this group of four then join with another group of four (becoming a group of eight) and share their reports with each other.

Example 3.8 Group work activity

Table 3.2 is an example of a group activity used by the author in training library and information professionals in the use of different training techniques.

Table 3.2 *Group work activity*	
Structure	**Content**
Learning outcome	To be able to evaluate different training techniques.
Process	In groups of four, identify the advantages and disadvantages of one of the following training techniques: presentations; group work; demonstrations; hands-on activity (prepare a list in advance that means that each group can lead on the feedback for one method). Prepare a summary which you will present to the whole group in 10 minutes.
Feedback	Ask a group to present its advantages/disadvantages for one of the methods. This could involve standing up and speaking with/without a flipchart/whiteboard. The group or the trainer can record key points. When the group has completed its feedback, ask everyone in the room if they have anything to add or any questions about the technique. Then move on to the next technique. Up to 5 minutes per technique.
End of activity	Thank everyone for their work.

TIP FOR TRAINERS

Beware of the so-called 'death by feedback'. This occurs when a trainer asks everyone in a group to report back and the process is repetitive and long winded. To avoid this situation, trainers may structure the reporting back in some way. For example:

- One person reports back from a table or group.
- Individuals are asked to add new points rather than repeat previous points.
- Ask everyone to give their report in no more than five words.

Guest speakers

Guest speakers are a means of helping to provide variety and change of pace in a training course. The guest speaker may be physically present or can visit using facilities such as Skype or video-conferencing, i.e. can be a virtual visitor. It is important to brief the guest before the event. One of the risks of inviting a guest speaker is that they may not follow your guidance. One method for managing guest speakers is to use an interview format.

Hands-on sessions

These are commonly used to teach individuals how to use specific computer-based systems, services or tools. A major factor that will affect the design of these sessions is the number of participants. If there are fewer than ten people, then it is normally possible to organize a more interactive session than if the group is very large, say 100 or 150 students.

A common method for organizing hands-on sessions is to use the following sequence of activities:

- introduction
- initial presentation
- practical hands-on activity using worksheets or online tutorials
- time for questions
- close.

Advantages:

- Individuals learn how to use the system by being actively engaged with it.
- It is possible to guide people through complicated procedures.
- Individuals can follow up their own interests.

Disadvantages:

- Individuals in a group may have different levels of experience and expertise.
- Individuals may ignore the trainer's guidance and use the time to keep up with their e-mails, Facebook, LinkedIn, etc.
- It can be difficult to control the group, e.g. when it is asked to complete an exercise, or to get it to pay attention to the trainer.

TIP FOR TRAINERS

- Standing at the back of the room will help you to assess everyone's progress.
- If you want to gain attention, then ask everyone to switch off their screens.
- Prepare a number of different handouts and activities so that you can meet the needs of people with varying levels of experience or expertise.

Ice-breakers

As their name suggests, ice-breakers help to 'break the ice' and relax people so that they can start concentrating and learning. They are particularly important if the learners don't know each other or are anxious about the training event. The purpose of ice-breakers is to:

- engage everyone with the training session
- help everyone to get to know each other
- establish a climate for learning.

It is important that the ice-breaker used by the trainer is acceptable to the group in terms both of the amount of time used for this activity and of the type of activity. Make sure that the amount of time spent is proportionate to the time–length of the whole training event. For example, in a one-day workshop it would be acceptable to spend ten minutes getting to know each other, but this would be unacceptable in a short, e.g. one-hour, training event. Some simple ice-breakers are outlined in Table 3.3.

Table 3.3 *Example ice-breakers*

Ice-breaker	Use
1. Introductions. Introduce yourself to everyone sitting at your table. Give your name, role and what you want to gain from the course. Timing 5 minutes. Then ask everyone to introduce themselves to the whole group by giving their name and what they want to gain from the training event. Trainer writes names and learning outcomes on a board. Timing – 10 minutes.	Groups of up to 18 when not everyone knows each other. Useful starting-point, as it gives everyone an opportunity to talk in their group and so to relax. Feedback to the whole group gives the trainer the opportunity to get to know everyone's names. The written record can be used as a reminder during the training event. At the end of the event, it can be used to ask participants whether or not they achieved their learning outcomes for the training.
2. Introductions – cascade. Ask everyone to introduce themselves to the person sitting next to them. Then, in the same pairs, each person must introduce their partner to another pair. Each group of four can then introduce themselves to another group of four. Timing – 10 minutes.	Very large groups, e.g. more than 20 participants. This helps individuals to meet up to eight people (or more, if the groups of eight then meet up with another group). In very large groups it is impossible to have introductions to the whole group but this technique does help to break the ice and means that groups of people know each other.
3. Bingo. Prepare a sheet with 6–12 general questions such as: 'Find one person who came to work by train – write their name on the sheet'. Hand out the sheets and ask everyone to complete the questions by talking to other people on the training session. The first person to complete the questions wins the game. A small prize can be awarded, if appropriate. Timing – 10 minutes.	Large groups, e.g. more than 12 people. Useful as an icebreaker and energizer. This activity helps to get people moving about and talking to each other. It can be useful at induction events when no one knows each other and people may be quite apprehensive.

Inquiry-based learning

This is a learning method where the focus is a real problem or situation, and this helps to stimulate learners' interest and engagement in the learning process. The term inquiry-based learning is used by different authors in slightly different ways and it may include problem-based learning, project-based learning and work-based learning. Kahn and O'Rourke (2005) identify the characteristics of inquiry-based learning as:

- Learners tackle complex problems or scenarios.
- Learners take charge of their learning process and decide on their lines of inquiry and their study methods.
- Learners use their existing knowledge, and also identify their learning needs.
- The learning tasks encourage the learners to search for new ideas or evidence.
- Learners take responsibility for presenting their findings, and also the supporting evidence and reasoning.

Figure 3.2 provides an illustration of inquiry-based learning; it is based on the work of Bruce and Davidson (1996).

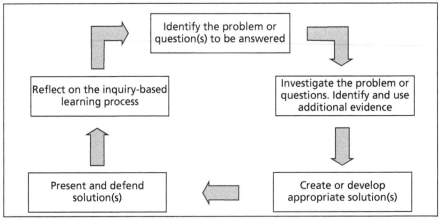

Figure 3.2 *Inquiry-based learning*

TIP FOR TRAINERS

If you are considering using inquiry-based learning, then think about your participants and their readiness for this approach to learning. How will you alert them to this approach? How will you help to structure or scaffold the process so that they understand the learning process and achieve the necessary learning outcomes?

Beware: if your participants are not clear about the value of this type of approach and the underlying pedagogy, then there is a danger that they may think the trainer is abdicating responsibility and leaving them to their own devices. ■

Lectures and presentations

Lectures and presentations are commonly used to provide an overview of a subject or theme. Typically they involve the trainer in providing an outline of the topic with the support of PowerPoint slides or other visual aids.

What are the advantages of lectures and presentations?

- They are a good method of providing an overview to a topic.
- They can be used to help a group to settle down and focus on the topic.
- They can be recorded – either audio or video – and made available via the internet.
- Some people expect them as part of a training programme.

What are the disadvantages of lectures and presentations?

- Some trainers attempt to put too much information across to their audience. This is the so-called 'death by PowerPoint'. It sometimes happens at inductions in higher education establishments when information skills tutors have an urge to provide students with as much information as possible, on the basis that they may not get another opportunity to do so.
- Concentration spans vary, and many people lose concentration after 20–30 minutes. This means that any presentation that lasts longer than 30 minutes needs to include a range of interactive activities in order to maintain motivation and interest in the topic.
- The trainer may find it difficult to control the group and may have to tackle issues such as talking, late arrivals, early departures, individuals using their mobile phones, etc.

A common structure for a lecture or presentation is as follows:

- review of housekeeping arrangements, including fire exits and evacuation procedure
- outline of the plan for the session
- introduction to the topic. Explain why it is important, and the benefits for the audience of learning about it. This will help motivate the audience
- outline of the topic. Explain what it is and provide some detail (but not too much detail)
- link to real-life practice. How does the topic relate to the audience in terms of what they need to be able to do?
- time for questions
- brief summary, e.g. of three key points from the lecture or presentation
- thank you to participants for listening, and end of session.

In terms of the break-down of time for a lecture or presentation, the following is a rough guide:

- introduction 10%
- main section 80%
- conclusion 10%.

Techniques for making lectures and presentations engaging include:

- keeping them brief
- using examples which are tailor-made for the specific audience
- using interactive exercises and activities
- making use of guest speakers and video clips
- using audience participation.

If you have decided to involve the audience actively, then you will need to decide what form the involvement will take and how it will fit into the presentation's structure. Example activities include: asking the audience to discuss a topic with their neighbour; asking them to complete some kind of questionnaire or take part in a quiz using an audience response system (see Chapter 4). You will need to think about how much time to spend on the activity and how you will intervene if the activity does not work.

Trainers also need to think about how they deal with questions in a lecture or presentation. It is up to you to decide when you will accept questions, e.g. during or at the end of a presentation. Inexperienced presenters often find it easier to take questions at the end of the presentation so as not to break their flow. Handling difficult questions is made easier by knowing that you are in control. The following general tips will help you to answer any type of question:

- Listen carefully to the question. You need to listen to the actual words and also the emotions behind the question. Often the body language of the questioner will give you some useful information.
- If you are not sure about the meaning of the question, then ask for clarification.
- Repeat the question in your own words. This will allow the whole audience to hear the question and it also allows you to check that you have fully understood the question.
- Answer the question to the best of your ability.
- If you don't know the answer, then be honest and say that you don't know. You may then want to ask if anyone in the audience can answer it, or you may offer to e-mail the answer.
- Signal how many questions you will take, e.g. at the end of your

presentation say that there is time for three or four questions.

• When you want to close the session, say that there is time for one more question and then after that question you must move on.

Table 3.4 provides a checklist which you can use to make sure that you have not overlooked something when preparing a lecture or presentation.

Table 3.4 *Checklist for preparing a lecture or presentation*	
Questions	Notes
What is the purpose of the lecture/presentation?	
What is the context of the lecture/presentation?	
Who are your audience and what is their current knowledge of the topic?	
What are their expectations from the lecture/presentation?	
How will the lecture/presentation be delivered? Will you be in the same room with the audience, or will your delivery be live online or recorded and made available via a podcast or other means?	
What length of time is available for the lecture or presentation? How can you make best use of it?	
How will you develop rapport with your audience?	
What is your main message?	
What other information do you need to convey in order to meet your objectives?	
What approach(es) could you use to present the topic and material in a clear, interesting and involving way?	
How formal or informal should your delivery of the material be?	
Is it appropriate to involve your audience in activities?	
How will you use technology within the lecture/presentation? What equipment will you have access to?	
What handouts, visual, audio or audiovisual aids could reinforce the content? When and how should they be used?	
How will you obtain audience feedback?	

Problem-based learning

Problem-based learning is a specific type of inquiry-based learning. It involves providing groups of learners with realistic scenarios or a problem situation which is then used to deliver the learning process. The problem, which is likely to be a complex one, may be a real-life one or may be one developed to ensure that the learners go through a particular learning experience. The learners may be presented with relevant data and information, or they may have either to generate their own data or to search for existing information. They then use this information to generate a solution or solutions to the problem. Finally, they are required to reflect on the problem-solving process and the lessons that they have learnt from it.

Savin-Baden (2007) describes the process of problem-solving learning as involving students or practitioners in working through the following stages, which involve both group and individual activities, and it may take place over a number of weeks or months:

1. Initial group activities:
   a. Study the problem.
   b. Identify what you need to know in order to solve the problem.
   c. Identify the group learning needs.
   d. Allocate the learning needs to individuals.
2. Individual activity:
   a. Research and achieve individual learning needs.
3. Group activities:
   a. Peer teaching of outcomes of individual research.
   b. Reassessment of overall goals in light of outcomes of individual research and group discussions.
   c. Formulation of action plan for managing or resolving the problem. This may result in the production of a specific output, e.g. proposal, factsheet, presentation or report.

This process is illustrated in Figure 3.3, which shows the timeline of students or practitioners working on a problem and using a wide range of resources and support facilities. The diagram also indicates the use of different technologies to support this process.

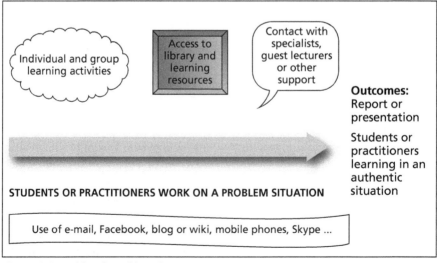

Figure 3.3 *Problem-based learning*

As with inquiry-based learning, if you are considering using problem-based learning, then think about your participants and their readiness for this approach. How will you alert them to this approach? How will you help to structure or scaffold the process so that they understand the learning process and achieve the necessary learning outcomes?

Beware: if your participants are not clear about the value of this type of approach and the underlying pedagogy, then there is a danger that they may think the trainer is abdicating responsibility and leaving them to their own devices.

Stories and metaphors

Stories and metaphors are a useful way of enlivening training sessions. They enable trainers to:

- provide inspiration
- illustrate a point
- introduce complex ideas
- by-pass the conscious mind
- energize participants
- provide a break
- change the pace or emotional climate of the training event.

Parkin (2010b) provides a useful guide to using stories and metaphors in support of learning and teaching. She provides the following guidance for thinking about their use in a training event:

1 What is the purpose of the story?
2 Does the story fit into the culture of the organization?
3 What type of story will be most appropriate – story from a book, personal anecdote, story from TV, film or other source?
4 What message is the trainer trying to convey?
5 How will the story fit into the session?

Parkin provides a detailed guide to using stories in training events, together with 50 example stories. An alternative to telling the story yourself is to obtain a short video clip of someone telling their story. These stories may be used a number of times, either in face-to-face sessions or in online training programmes.

Example 3.9 Telling stories

I regularly use stories in my training courses. As I work in an academic environment, these often come from students' experiences. As an audience, students love stories about their peers' successes and failures. Clearly, the identity of the person at the centre of a story needs to be disguised, but stories about students failing their module, year or even whole degree as a result of plagiarism and poor academic referencing normally engage their full attention.

Surveys and questionnaires

Questionnaires or surveys may be used in a number of different ways and at different stages in the training process, as indicated below:

- pre-training session
  — diagnostic quiz
  — finding out about delegates' needs
- on the course
  — diagnostic quiz
  — assessment activity
- end of session
  — evaluation.

Important points about the use of questionnaires include:

- How do they help you to achieve your learning outcome(s)?
- Is their length appropriate (a 20-question survey may take 15–20 minutes to complete)?
- Is their language appropriate for the participants?
- Will you provide pencils or pens (for paper-based surveys)?
- What will you do if some people complete them very quickly while others take a long time?
- How will you report back on the results?

The internet provides access to tools which allow you to design and deliver online questionnaires (see Chapter 4), and it also provides access to many examples of questionnaires and surveys. Some interesting examples can be found on the following websites:

- learning styles quizzes
  — suitable for school pupils,
    www.brainboxx.co.uk/a3_aspects/pages/vak_quest.htm
  — suitable for adults,
    http://www.open.edu/openlearn/education/educational-technology-
    and-practice/educational-practice/whats-your-learning-style
    www.engr.ncsu.edu/learningstyles/ilsweb.html
- plagiarism quizzes
  — USA High School example which includes an honour statement,
    www.mtlsd.org/highschool/highschoolplagiarismlessons.asp

— UK university example, www.uea.ac.uk/menu/admin/dos/quiz/
— USA university example,
   https://www.indiana.edu/~tedfrick/plagiarism/index2.html
- study skills quizzes
  — UK university example,
     www2.hull.ac.uk/student/studyadvice/studyskillsresources/quizzes.aspx
  — Australian university example, www.newcastle.edu.au/service/connect-
     2-success/quizzes/study-skills.html
  — publisher example, www.palgrave.com/skills4study/

Clearly, if you wish to use someone else's quiz, then you need to seek and obtain their permission.

Treasure hunts

Treasure hunts are a useful means of enabling groups of library users, e.g. pupils or students, to explore the library and information service in a structured manner. Essentially, they are self-guided tours which include an element of fun and competition.

Treasure hunts are commonly used in educational institutions as a means of helping new pupils or students to learn their way around the campus and library.

Advantages:
- Treasure hunts enable relatively large groups of students to find their way around a library and identify key features.
- They are sometimes the only way of managing the induction needs of very large groups.
- They encourage pupils or students to socialize with each other and also to share their knowledge of the library.
- They are fun.

Disadvantages:
- Some pupils or students may perceive them as patronizing.
- The pupils or students are out of sight and may choose to ignore the treasure hunt and go off on their own.
- They take time to plan and pilot.

Case study 3.3 Using a treasure hunt in induction

Figure 3.4 is an example of a treasure hunt used in a university business school during the induction of undergraduate students where there were typically 500 students in each cohort. Although many of the questions are simple, they did require students to walk around the campus and library and identify key features. Overall, this activity worked well and the majority of students engaged with it.

Treasure Hunt
The purpose of this activity is twofold: to enable you to start to get to know your colleagues on the course; and to enable you to find your way around the campus. What you should do:
1 Get into groups of three or four students.
2 As a group, work your way around the campus answering the following questions.
3 When you have completed the questionnaire hand it in to _____
4 A prize will be given for the first correct questionnaire to be pulled out of the box.

Questions	
1 How many computers are available for undergraduate students on the 1st floor of the Brookside Building?	
2 How do you obtain help with technology in the 1st floor computer room in the Brookside Building?	
3 In which building is the Computer Centre?	
4 What are the opening hours of the Help Desk in the Computer Centre?	
5 What time does the library open in the morning?	
6 Does the library open on a Sunday?	
7 How many self-service machines are there at the Issue Counter in the library?	
8 On which floor of the library are the new periodicals kept?	
9 Where is the Study Advice Service in the library?	
10 Does the Study Advice Service offer help with referencing?	
11 What is the view from the window in the business and management section on the third floor?	
12 Do you need a student card to use the library catalogue?	
13 Is it possible to reserve books while at home in bed?	
14 Is it possible to read a paper copy of The Economist in the library?	
15 Is it possible to read an electronic copy of The Economist via the library website while at home in bed?	
16 What services are available to students on the top floor of the library?	
17 How do you obtain access to copies of exam papers in the library?	
18 What services are available to students in the basement of the library?	
19 Is it possible to borrow DVDs of films from the library?	
20 What is the name of the business librarian?	

Figure 3.4 *Treasure hunt*

Using a combination of methods

Trainers frequently use a combination of training methods and move between different approaches, depending on their group and their experiences of working with a particular group. This is demonstrated in the following example and case study. Additional examples of the use of a number of different training methods are considered in the following chapters.

Example 3.10 Using different training methods

Harding (2012), writing in the context of training with respect to school libraries says:

People learn in different ways. They also need variety during a course in order to keep interested, alert and receptive. For both these reasons I use a diversity of training methods in all my courses. Almost everyone learns more effectively if they are actively engaged, so this is my guiding principle. Following a brief introduction, I quickly involve everyone in small-group discussion on some important aspect of the training topic. Group work and plenary discussions are the cornerstones of my courses. If I observe that some individuals find it hard to join in and are shy about speaking even in small groups, I may include pair work. Group and pair work enables delegates to share good practice and learn from each other in a supportive environment. I include practical tasks or activities where possible, for example a book-related activity in courses on children's reading, with guidance on aspects to explore. Attention levels are always at their lowest after lunch, so that's the time I choose for practical elements. I use lots of visual stimuli for learning on courses: pictures, photographs and, where appropriate, video footage. On courses where it is important to impart lots of knowledge, I use dialogue rather than lecturing. A précis backed up with detailed hand-outs is better than a long discourse.

Case study 3.4 Incorporating a range of training methods into induction training on a busy campus

This case study provided by Mires (2012) illustrates the range of awareness-raising and training methods used to deliver library induction during orientation week, when library staff are dealing with very large groups of students, at the University of Westminster's Marylebone site:

QR Codes

As QR (Quick Response) codes enable the connection of physical and virtual information, they were considered a useful tool for enhancing tours and highlighting the library's virtual presence. The codes were incorporated as part of a short tour that could be delivered as a group or self-guided activity. Ideas for the tour were chosen because they would be quick and easy to create using information already readily available, physical objects could then be linked to virtual information by means of the QR codes.

Cephalonia method

The Cephalonia method of library instruction/orientation originated from Cardiff University Library staff. It was designed to introduce engagement and student participation into library presentations. Colour-coded cards with questions on them are distributed to the audience at the beginning of the session. During the session students are encouraged to ask questions from their cards, and these are answered by a correlated slide in the presentation. The method was identified as a suitable way of presenting information to international students.

It was thought to be appropriate for the general introductory information that would be presented prior to site-/subject-based orientation. The spontaneous style of the method also aided interaction and elicited further questions.

Multimedia clip

Research into orientation methods at other institutions highlighted the advantages of using a mixture of media when presenting information. A multimedia clip was produced in collaboration with AV staff and used in lecture-theatre/classroom sessions to replace physical tours and to add another dimension to textual/oral information. The final clip was shown during orientation sessions outside of the library, and proved to be very popular with both academics and students. When the clip becomes available online this can also be viewed by students who have missed orientation.

www.youtube.com/watch?v=G8FEIF-mR6w&feature=plcp

Welcome space

The library space at Marylebone lacked an area where students could gather and locate library and IT orientation information at the start of term. The spaces on the first floor were assessed, and an area of redundant shelving units close to the counter was identified as a suitable space to develop. The following publicity and information items were displayed in the area for the duration of orientation:

- welcome posters
- business cards
- merchandise – pencils and pens
- 'What your Academic Liaison Librarian/IT trainer can do for you' flyers
- 'Introduction to Blackboard' leaflets
- schedule of drop-in sessions for semester one
- QR trail flyers
- QR posters (to scan as part of trail)
- 'Library Search' leaflets.

Having a specific space to which to direct students for orientation purposes was useful, although we still need to monitor it and evaluate whether students have the same perception of it. The Welcome Space can also be used as a more permanent area for showcasing services and resources that students should be aware of and to raise their visibility.

TIP FOR TRAINERS

Once you have produced an outline course plan, ask yourself the following questions:

- Will course participants find this interesting?
- Will I find it interesting to deliver?

- Have I used a range of learning and teaching methods?
- Will participants be involved in different types of activities during the course?
- Would I like to attend this course?

Summary

This chapter has provided an overview of different methods of delivering learning and teaching. While not exhaustive it covers methods commonly used by trainers. These training methods can be combined to produce an engaging, relevant and dynamic training event or programme. Additional training methods which involve the use of ICTs are described in Chapter 4, and Chapter 8 provides a guide to over 90 workplace learning activities which may be incorporated into training programmes. Chapter 5 provides guidance on designing training programmes building on the examples covered in this chapter.

References and additional resources

Brockband, A. and McGill, I. (2012) *Facilitating Reflective Learning*, Kogan Page.

Bruce, B.C. and Davidson, J. (1996) An Inquiry Model for Literacy Across the Curriculum, *Journal of Curriculum Studies*, **28**, 281–300.

Fee, K. (2011) *101 Learning and Development Tools*, Kogan Page.

Harding, A. (2012) Personal communication.

Herrington, J., Reeves, T. C. and Oliver, R. (2009) *A Guide to Authentic E-learning*, Routledge.

Iverson, K. (2004) *E-learning Games*, Pearson.

Kahn, P. and O'Rourke, K. (2005) Understanding Enquiry-based Learning (EBL). In Barret, T., Labhrainn, I. and Fallon, H. (eds), *Handbook of Enquiry and Problem-based Learning: Irish case studies and international perspectives*, Galwa, CELT.

Mires, E. (2012) *Personal communication.*

Moust, J., Bouhuijs, P. and Schmidt, H. (2007) *Introduction to Problem-based Learning*, Routledge.

Parkin, M. (2010a) *More Tales for Trainers*, Kogan Page.

Parkin, M. (2010b) *Tales for Trainers*, Kogan Page.

Parkin, M. (2010c) *Tools for Change*, Kogan Page.

Pike, B. and Solem, L. (2000) *50 Creative Training Openers and Energizers: innovative ways to start your training with a bang!*, Wiley.

Savin-Baden, M. (2007) *A Practical Guide to Problem-based Learning Online*, Routledge.

Smith, A.-L. and Baker, L. (2011) Getting a Clue: creating student detectives and dragon slayers in your library, *Reference Services Review*, **39** (4), 628–42.

Sugar, S. (1998) *Games that Teach Teams: 21 activities to super-charge your group*, Wiley.

4

Use of different technologies to support training practices

Introduction

One of the challenges in writing this chapter is the speed of technological development and the continuing availability of new tools and techniques to support training activities. Consequently, this chapter focuses on providing a general overview of the different ways in which current technologies can be incorporated into training programmes.

Initially, the internet provided library and information trainers with access to a range of tools and facilities to support learning and teaching. These included:

- web-based tutorials
- online communication tools
  - asynchronous tools such as discussion boards and messaging services
  - synchronous tools such as chat or meeting rooms
- specialist software which could be used to develop games, quizzes and surveys, presentations, multimedia resources.

In educational institutions, these were often combined to produce virtual learning environments (VLEs) such as Blackboard and WebCT, which also included online tracking systems.

The rise of social media and Web 2.0 has provided an increased range of tools that may be used for learning and development. At first sight, these appear to be a complex array, but they can be divided into three main groups: communication tools, collaboration tools, and multimedia. Common examples are presented in Table 4.1.

Keeping up to date is a real challenge. New technologies appear to be developed at an ever-increasing speed and trends and patterns of use are constantly changing.

Table 4.1 *Social media tools (adapted from Cann, Dimitriou and Hooley, 2011)*

Function	Type of tool	Specific examples
Communication	Aggregator	Google Reader, Netvibes, Pageflakes
	Blogging	Blogger, LiveJournal, Typepad, WordPress
	Microblogging	Twitter, Yammer
	Social networking	Facebook, LinkedIn
Collaboration	Conferencing	GoToMeeting, Skype
	Meetings	Adobe ConnectNow, Groupboard, Google Groups, ShowMyPC
	Project management	Joyent, Project2Manage
	Social bibliography	CitULike, Mendeley
	Social bookmarking	Delicious, Diigo
	Social documents	Google Docs, Dropbox
	Social news	Digg, reddit, Newsvine
	Wiki	PBworks, Wetpaint, Wikia
Multimedia	Live streaming	Justin.tv, Livestream
	Photographs	Flickr, Picasa
	Presentation sharing	SlideShare
	Virtual world	Second Life

TIP FOR TRAINERS

A valuable source for keeping up to date in the library world is the website of Phil Bradley at www.philb.com. In addition he regularly produces useful books which provide an up-to-date summary of a particular aspect of technology.

This chapter is devoted to exploring both 'traditional' internet learning and teaching facilities and real-time media tools. They are arranged in alphabetical order.

Apps

Apps (or application software) are available online from a variety of sources and they may be run on computers, laptops and tablets, smartphones and other electronic devices. Apps rose to fame when Apple launched the iPhone 3G in 2008, and the Apple App Store popularized the idea of downloading applications and application updates from a single website. Apple now provides more than half a million apps from its App store. Apps are available from many websites, e.g. Microsoft, BBC, and may be available free or for a charge. Library and information services can develop their own apps to support learning and teaching and there are numerous websites available which provide the necessary tools. For example:

- AppsBuilder, www.apps-builder.com/
- Appmakr, www.appmakr.com/
- Buildanapp, www.buildanapp.com/home
- Buzztouch, www.buzztouch.com/

- OpenPlug, www.openplug.com
- Widgetbox, www.widgetbox.com.

Example 4.1 Apps for librarian productivity

Goldsmith writes on the Infopeople blog (see www.infoblog.infopeople.org/2012/):

> First off, I use my iPad for both work and play. I teach online courses from it, develop curriculum on it, file as well as read email, Tweets and assorted blog-posted sites I think warrant return visits. I move around a lot while I work so the iPad travels in my small backpack .... In other words, my iPad is a practical extension of my hands as well as my workspace.

She then describes in some detail the apps that she uses, including Pages, SynchSpace, Skitch, Flipboard, Keynote and iBooks.

Audience response systems

An audience response system (also called a student response system or personal response system) provides a means for a group of people (the audience) to provide feedback to a trainer or presenter. The basic idea is that the trainer uses a computer and data projector to give a presentation which incorporates questions which the audience answer as the session progresses, using their clickers or keypads. These systems normally work using wireless technologies. A commonly used system in educational institutions is the TurningPoint Audience Response System. Its website provides tutorials, videos, discussion groups and technical support. Some audience response systems work by using mobile phones and collecting SMS responses and displaying them through a web page.

Advantages of audience response systems:

- They provide a means of obtaining feedback from the audience.
- They encourage interaction and engagement with the session.
- They provide a means of assessing learning.
- Polls can be anonymous, so individuals don't stand out if they get an answer right or wrong.
- With some systems, the responses can be linked to individuals and recorded, e.g. in a VLE.
- The results can be displayed immediately on the screen.
- People are familiar with these systems, as a result of their use in TV game shows.

Disadvantages of audience response systems include:

- the cost of the equipment

- the time required to work out the questions and set up the presentation
- the time required to hand out and collect in the clickers (for mobile systems).

Example 4.2 Using an audience response system with medical students

Kanesho et al. (2008) describe the use of an audience response system as a means of measuring medical students' understanding of literature retrieval techniques and to understand their information-seeking habits. Using the system helped to make the sessions productive and positively received by the students.

Case study 4.1 Using an audience response system with engineering students

Bush (2010, 7) describes using an audience response system to conduct library orientations with engineering students. She writes:

> My biggest challenge with using the audience response system was writing good questions. In my opinion, the technology would have added more value if my questions had been better ... An audience response system can make a lecture format more palatable for engineering students and provide a way to engage their attention, thus making it more likely that they will retain some information.

Audio files

An audio file is a sound file which can be produced using a variety of devices, including a mobile phone, MP3 player or similar. The file can then be e-mailed to learners or made available to them via a VLE, blog or wiki. See also Podcasts.

Advantages of using audio files are that they:

- are quick and easy to make
- are easy to disseminate
- have a common format
- are accessible to individuals with some disabilities.

Disadvantages of using audio files include:

- It takes a little practice to become confident in using this medium.
- Individuals receiving the audio file will need to have access to basic IT equipment with a sound card in order to listen to it.

Audio files are relevant to trainers as they may be used to:

- provide feedback

- provide an update
- welcome participants to a forthcoming event
- record part of a presentation.

Case study 4.2 Student welcome

I used an audio file as a means of recording a welcome to students who were due to attend a lecture on referencing. The file was less than three minutes long. I used it to introduce myself and put over the idea that the lecture would help the students to do well in their assignments. In the lecture, I asked how many students had listened to the file (sent by e-mail). Just over 50% had accessed it. Overall, it seemed to help the session to get off to a good start.

Blogs

A 'blog' or weblog is a popular method of keeping in touch, e.g. with colleagues or customers. Individuals write blogs as a means of sharing information and ideas. Blogs are very simple to create and there are many free online blogging tools, such as Blogger, WordPress and Livejournal. Some organizations, e.g. universities and colleges, provide staff and students with access to a blogging service. Alternatively, there are blogging services which require a paid subscription, and these provide a better service and more tools than the free ones. For most people's purposes, the free blogging tools are sufficient.

It is a good idea to look at a number of blogs before you consider starting your own. Some good examples include:

- Sheila Webber's Information Literacy Weblog at http://information-literacy.blogspot.co.uk/
- Phil Bradley's information technologies blog at www.philb.com
- Moira Bent's Infolit blog at www.moirabent.blogspot.co.uk
- Law Librarian Blog at www.lawprofessors.typepad.com/law_librarian_blog/
- Lori Reed: a work in progress at www.lorireed.com.

Blogs are normally text based but they can include images, videos, hyperlinks, movies and uploaded files. Entries are organized in date order (most recent first) and are automatically archived (in an accessible archive) once a month. An RSS or Twitter feed can be embedded in the blog and it is quite common for the blogging tool to produce a tag cloud, i.e. an image of the most popular keywords (or tags) from each blog post. Many blogs provide tools that enable readers to add their own comments. In addition to public blogs, it is possible to set up private or restricted-access blogs with some blogging tools.

Advantages of blogs:

- commonly used tools

- easy to use
- free tools are available.

Disadvantages of blogs:

- It takes time to design and develop a blog.
- They must be updated at regular intervals, e.g. at least weekly.
- Individuals may not interact with the blog by adding their own comments.
- It is easy to produce an unprofessional-looking blog.

The following list provides examples of the use of blogs to support training activities:

- to share ideas and update colleagues or others about new developments or resources in a specific field, e.g. as a current awareness tool
- to share the experience of attending a professional conference or study tour
- to record continuous professional development, e.g. a reflective journal
- to capture and record the lessons learnt during a project
- as a learning tool, e.g. small groups of school pupils or students could be asked to develop a blog on a specific theme, such as information sources on a particular topic, plagiarism, use of the library
- in academic programmes, blogs are increasingly used as an assessment tool and students are required to produce either an individual or group blog on a specific topic, or to use a blog to develop an individual learning journal.

TIP FOR TRAINERS

If you develop and use a blog, then remember that it is rather like a long-distance race – you need to keep it going through thick and thin. The internet is awash with blogs which were started enthusiastically and then fizzled out. You need to keep it updated and post regular entries. Strategies for helping you to do this include: putting it in your online calendar as a regular (e.g. weekly) activity, asking customers or course participants to get involved or asking colleagues to post entries too. ▨

Games

Whitton and Moseley (2012, 197) write: 'games can be an effective tool to support and enhance learning and teaching in a variety of educational settings and contexts. However, their use is not without its drawbacks, and there are a number of major challenges that we see in the field that need to be overcome before the use of games in learning can achieve its potential.'

Games are a powerful method of introducing fun, changing pace or helping people to focus, e.g. after a refreshment or lunch break. There are many tools available on the internet, which makes it very easy to produce simple games such as anagrams, word puzzles or crosswords. Phil Bradley provides a useful summary of Web 2.0 tools for education at www.philb.com and many of the tools which he cites are useful for developing training materials and activities with school children. Further guidance on using games in training is provided in Chapter 3.

Some useful URLs for different types of games are:

- anagram generator, http://wordsmith.org/anagram/
- tool for producing a number of puzzles, http://puzzlemaker.discoveryeducation.com/choosepuzzle
- crossword puzzles, www.armoredpenguin.com/crossword/
- word search puzzles, www.armoredpenguin.com/wordsearch/
- word scramble puzzles, www.armoredpenguin.com/wordscramble/.

Advantages of using internet-based games tools include:

- They are easy to use.
- Many free tools are available.
- They have commonly used formats, e.g. word search, crossword puzzles.
- They provide a break and a change in training sessions.
- They can be completed individually or in pairs.
- They can be used to introduce competition or fun.

Disadvantages of using internet-based games tools include:

- Not everyone enjoys games, or games based on the use of text.
- It takes time to learn how to use the online tool, and also to prepare the game.

Case study 4.3 Use of crosswords in a public library training session

Andreos, a librarian working in a public library in the USA, developed a crossword puzzle for use at the beginning of his training sessions. He used a free online tool to make the puzzle.[1] He worked in a rural public library and staff often arrived very early for his sessions. He put a copy of the crossword on everyone's chair before the start of the session and early arrivals often started filling it in and chatting with others as they arrived. He then gave everyone a chance to complete it just before lunch and then reviewed it after lunch. He used this technique quite regularly and found that it gave early arrivals something to focus on.

TIP FOR TRAINERS

If you develop and use any games using online tools, then keep them simple and test the games with friends and colleagues.

Interactive whiteboards

An interactive whiteboard, sometimes called an IWB or smartboard, is a touch-sensitive whiteboard normally mounted on a wall that allows students and their trainers to participate interactively in taught sessions. It consists of three pieces of equipment: a computer, a data projector and the touch-sensitive screen. The computer can be controlled from the whiteboard, e.g. by pointing at icons with a finger, by using a special electronic 'pen', or via a keyboard or mouse. These actions are then transmitted to the computer.

Interactive whiteboards are particularly useful for demonstrations to the whole group. Individuals can be asked to come to the board and edit what is on the screen. In the UK, they are very common in schools. In the context of library and information work, interactive whiteboards can be used to:

- demonstrate searching techniques, e.g. library catalogue, commercial database or the internet
- encourage reading and enhance literacy skills.

Example 4.3 Interactive whiteboards in an Australian school library

Measday (2006) describes the use of whiteboards in an Australian school library and uses photographs of students in a library which are projected onto a whiteboard as a means to engage them in discussions and activities about behaviours. She also uses them as a tool for teaching information literacy and study skills, e.g. note taking. In addition, she uses them to build up character maps or thought maps using software such as Inspire. She describes many other applications in her article.

Mind mapping

Mind mapping is the term coined by Tony Buzan to describe a visual means of presenting and organizing information. Nowadays many examples are available on the internet of software which enables you to produce mind maps for free, e.g. FreeMind (see freemind.sourceforge.net/). In addition, it is possible to subscribe to some services in order to access more sophisticated features.

Mind maps can be used as part of a training programme for individual or group activities in order to:

- develop or organize ideas
- develop and produce a plan, e.g. for a training session
- summarize learning at the end of a training session.

Alternatively, paper-based mind maps can be produced by individuals or groups as part of a training event.

Mobile learning

Mobile devices such as smartphones, tablets or other portable media devices are rapidly developing and provide increasing opportunities for trainers. They can be incorporated into training events as a means of engaging individuals before, during or after the event. This is a rapidly changing market and each successive wave of mobile devices provides increased facilities and functions. Below are some basic ideas about how different mobile technologies can be used for learning and teaching. Smartphones are now commonly used by many people as an essential everyday tool. JISC has carried out research in this area in its MoRSE project.[2]

In the context of training and development they can be used to:

- access VLEs and websites
- access apps
- read news feeds delivered by RSS
- record presentations or interviews (both audio and video)
- take photographs
- take brief notes
- take part in brief quizzes
- send e-mails and SMS messages
- contribute to on-screen instant messaging, e.g. as part of a presentation
- engage in videoconferencing
- work collaboratively through a VLE or social networking sites such as LinkedIn.

However, there are disadvantages to using these technologies as part of a training programme:

- Everyone participating in the activity needs to have access to the technology.
- It may be expensive (depending on individual contracts).
- Some organizations limit the uses of smartphones by their staff, e.g. many companies don't permit access to social networking sites or apps.
- They are not very good for work which requires writing lengthy items, reading articles or other long materials.

Tablet devices include the Apple iPad, Samsung Galaxy Tab and Blackberry Playbook, which all provide access to the internet and a range of tools and functions. Tablet devices can be used for all of the functions listed above for smartphones. In addition, they can be used to produce lengthy documents (provided that you have the appropriate software) and to store files and other resources, e.g. multimedia. Their main advantages are that they are relatively light, easy to read and often offer high-specification functionality. However, they are relatively expensive to purchase and you normally have to send your files to another computer (or to a wireless printer) in order to print them out.

E-readers are small, hand-held devices which enable one to download and read books, and also to carry out some other functions, e.g. use e-mail and websites. Individual companies provide e-readers, e.g. the online bookstore Amazon provides the Kindle, and the number and range of books and other resources available for e-readers is growing rapidly. However, many specialist books are not available as e-books. This is a rapidly changing field and one that is well worth watching, as educational institutions are beginning to invest in the production of materials in e-book formats and the provision to their students of e-books containing course materials. JISC has carried out research in this area in the Duckling project.[3]

Example 4.4 Using mobile devices for induction and library orientation

Mobile devices are becoming increasingly common as a means of helping new library users to find their way around the library (mobile tours), to provide library guides, to organize treasure or scavenger hunts or to provide additional information on posters (using QR codes). They can be used to augment or replace traditional methods. Some interesting case studies are available at www.m-libraries.info/2012/.

Podcasts

A podcast is a downloadable sound or video file. Podcasts can be useful for providing welcomes, instructions, library tours, summaries or additional help or explanations in an e-learning or blended learning programme. Video podcasts are sometimes called vodcasts.

Podcasts can be produced using a wide range of devices, including mobile phones, dictation machines, laptops and tablets. Interviews, e.g. with guest speakers or authors, can be recorded as podcasts. It is important to keep them short – two or three minutes is long enough. If you have a long recording, then split it into separate files.

Some useful websites for podcasts include:

- Apple's educational podcast site, iTunesU,
  www.apple.com/education/itunes-u/
- A useful guide to the use of podcasts using iTunes,
  www.apple.com/itunes/podcasts
- Audio editing software (free), http://audacity.sourceforge.net

---

Case study 4.4 A sound education: using podcasts to develop study skills

Croft, Maxwell and Scopes (2011) describe the production of podcasts to support students' learning. They produced podcasts in the areas of plagiarism, essay writing and data analysis. They used unscripted recordings, as their experience was that these came over as more authentic and engaging than scripted recordings, and they used a discussion format as a means of presenting the material. They also experimented with recording student interviews and obtaining their views on time management. Overall, the use of podcasts was popular and their first eight podcasts were listened to more than 2500 times (approximately 300 hours of listening).

See: Leeds Metropolitan University, Skills for Learning (website) [accessed 25 November 2010].[4]

TIP FOR TRAINERS

I love podcasts and video clips! They are quick and easy to develop and produce. I use my mobile phone to make short recordings, e.g. of colleagues, students, employers and others. Two to five minutes is long enough. Many people are so used to YouTube that you don't need to worry about producing a top-class recording. ▨

PowerPoint

Microsoft's PowerPoint is one of the most commonly used presentation packages and it is a useful tool for the following reasons:

- familiar tool and commonly available
- simple to use
- can be linked to websites and video clips
- advanced features available
- printouts are possible in a variety of formats.

Basic rules of using PowerPoint:

- Don't overuse.
- Typically, 10–15 slides for an hour-long presentation is sufficient.
- Have no more than seven lines per slide and seven words per line.
- Use images, video clips and other features to enhance the presentation.

When presenting with PowerPoint:

- Don't read from the slides.
- Use the slides as a general guide and 'add value' to them through your comments and stories.
- Provide your audience with a copy of the presentation either before or after the session.

QR codes

A QR code is the name given to a two-dimensional barcode (or matrix barcode) which can be downloaded onto a mobile phone (or other smart mobile device). QR readers are available as apps for many smartphones with a built-in camera and web browser. QR codes can be generated relatively simply by accessing sites such as: http://qrcode.kaywa.com/ and http://incn.eu/. They can be used to store website URLs, text, phone numbers, e-mail addresses or any other alphanumeric data. An internet link to a library guide can be converted into a QR code and the guide can then be accessed and downloaded by readers using their mobile phones. Similarly, a library plan may be linked via a QR code to an audio tour. QR codes can be used to add additional information to a poster or handout. A useful resource on QR codes is available at www.m-libraries.info.

Example 4.5 Using QR codes to develop a scavenger hunt in a school library

An interesting example of the use of QR codes is presented in a blog which is based on a middle school teacher-librarian's experience in the USA (written by Gwyneth Anne Bronwynne Jones and called 'The Daring Librarian').[5] Jones developed a Scavenger Hunt aimed at middle school pupils. This involved groups of pupils using smartphones to access QR codes posted around the library in order to find the answers to a set of questions.

Screen recording

It is very useful to be able to record what is on your screen and then incorporate it into a PowerPoint presentation or video as a learning resource. There are many software tools available which can be used for screen recording. Examples include: Grab, GoView, ScreenToaster and Snagit. The specific facilities of screen-recording software vary, as indicated in the following two examples:

- Grab (an Apple product – see www.apple.com/macosx) is very typical of this type of software and it will enable you to grab part of the screen or the entire screen, or the window. It also has a delayed action function.
- Snagit (see www.techsmith.com/snagit) is a screen-shot capture program that captures video displays and audio output. It has an extensive range of features which enable trainers to develop and produce high-quality products.

Case study 4.5 Students' preferences for tutorial design: a usability study

Mestre (2012) provides an interesting study of her evaluation of whether students performed better after working with a screencast library tutorial or a web-based tutorial with static screen-shots. A screencast tutorial was produced using software such as Captivate, Wink or CamStudio which captures whatever is on the screen (e.g. working through an online search), and has options for adding captions, highlights, audio voice-over, quizzes, etc. This can be disseminated via e-mail, VLEs or a website. In contrast, a web-based tutorial with static screen-shots provides a rather one-dimensional learning experience, and although it is possible to incorporate sound, images, quizzes, etc. this is often much more technically complicated (and therefore time consuming) than using screencasting (or grabbing) software. Feedback from the students was interesting (and contradictory), as is demonstrated by the following quotations:

> On the video tutorial I liked to see the mouse actually move and click, and the highlighting and the pop-ups.

> The text-based one [web-based tutorial] is easiest to go back and forth with and to get the whole picture and then the details.
>
> (Mestre, 2012, 265–6)

Overall, the study indicated that students wanted to control their pace and route through the learning materials and that they liked the option in the web-based tutorial to go back and double-check their understanding. In addition, the availability of multimedia in these tutorials enhanced the students' experiences.

Mestre (2012; 271–3) provides some general guidelines for creating effective library tutorials, which take into account learning styles theories. The main points include:

- Create a good outline and navigation.
- Provide clear and detailed images.
- Use appropriate multimedia.
- Highlight salient points.
- Keep text to a minimum.
- Provide an easy way to work through the tutorial:
  — Provide flexible models of informal self-assessment.
  — Provide opportunities to practise with support.
  — Make activities easy to complete without help or explanations and use worked examples.
- Make the experience personal and relevant.
- Present information in chunks and in multiple formats.
- Provide options for novices and advanced learners.
- Provide ongoing, relevant feedback.

TIP FOR TRAINERS

Record your online search and keep it as a back-up to live searches. If the system goes down, then you can quickly switch presentations to 'here is one I prepared earlier'.

Screen sharing

There are many tools available which will enable you to share your computer screen with someone else, e.g. Crossloop, Radmin, UltraVNC or Yugma. These are useful in training, particularly if you are working with someone at a distance, as they share their screen with you and you can demonstrate specific tools or functions, or help them to deal with technical issues.

Case study 4.6 Database searching

Marcus worked in a pharmaceutical company and was having difficulty searching a database while he was visiting a supplier in Germany. He contacted his information specialist, who used screen-sharing software to diagnose the problem and advise Marcus on how to complete his search.

Skype

See Web conferencing.

Social networking tools

Social networking sites such as Facebook and LinkedIn provide a means of establishing a community of interest (individuals interested in the same professional area); making contact with other professionals; exchanging information, ideas, media; finding out about new jobs.

Joining such a network is normally simple, easy and free – you will need to provide your e-mail address and a password. If you establish your own pages, then you need to provide some additional information about yourself, and it is worth checking on the privacy facilities offered by the parent site. Some organizations block access to these sites while others support their usage for genuine professional reasons. Traditionally, Facebook has always been a site for personal networking and LinkedIn a professional one; however, the boundaries between personal and professional can become unclear on social networking sites and there are regular newspaper stories about individuals who have had their professional lives damaged, due to their inappropriate use of social networking sites such as Facebook.

Surveys or questionnaires

While many organizations have their own in-house questionnaire or survey tools, there are many that are available via the internet. One of the most commonly used tools is Survey Monkey (www.surveymonkey.com). This is easy to use and a simple e-mail to participants which includes a link to the survey is all that is required when asking anyone to complete the survey. Clearly, time needs to be spent on designing and piloting the survey so as to ensure that it works.

TIP FOR TRAINERS

Surveys are over-used in the workplace and in educational institutions. If you decide to use one, then keep it short.

Anything comprising more than about 10 questions is too long, and if you ask 2 to 4 questions you may get a much better response rate.

Find out if other surveys are being sent out at the same time that you want to post yours – many people suffer from survey fatigue.

Twitter

Twitter is an online service, essentially a social networking text messaging tool, which enables individuals to send and receive short messages (tweets) of up to 140 characters. It is very easy to set up, as all you need to do is sign up at www.twitter.com, providing your name, e-mail address and a password, and then follow the instructions. It is possible to send and receive tweets via smartphones, tablets and laptops, as well as PCs. Tweets can be sent to anyone; if you establish a closed group, they will be seen only by people to whom you have given permission. This is very useful in terms of library training practice, as you may wish to set up a closed group for a particular training event or group of customers.

Phil Bradley writes on his blog (www.philb.com/articles):

> So, a few useful reasons for keeping Twitter – news; global, national, local, professional, personal. Links to images, video, long posts, polls, event curation. Very flexible and reasonably easy to use.
>
> A few reasons for not using it – a deluge of never ending tweets, a lack of continuity caused by the 140 limit, an uncertainty over the value or authority of the information, the potential for mischief.

How can Twitter support training?

- Use it to inform people or remind them about forthcoming and imminent training events.
- Use it to send useful links.
- Use it to obtain feedback, e.g. during or after a training event.
- Use it to inform people about new resources or guides linked to a training event.
- Use it to market your training events.
- Use it to socialize and send out informal 'stuff' too – this will encourage the development of a community of library followers.
- Use it as a means of communicating with other library and information workers, and keeping up with training ideas.

Videos

Nowadays it is possible to create videos cheaply and easily using tools such as mobile phones and relatively cheap hand-held video recorders. Short videos, e.g. two to six minutes long, can be used to support training activities in a number of different ways:

- in a web-based tutorial
- as a 'trigger' to engage participants' interest, e.g. e-mail participants a link to the trigger video before a training event
- to liven up a training session.

Example 4.6 Movie magic: the thrill of Hollywood enhances information literacy teaching at Cardiff

Jones, Morgan, Nicholas and Swain (2011) provide an entertaining account of the challenges involved in producing four videos or movies on different aspects of information literacy. They developed four movies to add to their Information Literacy Resource Bank (ILRB) and these were produced with the aid of students and an academic, as well as a media production team. They can be viewed at http://ilrb.cf.ac.uk.

Virtual learning environments

A VLE is now an established feature in colleges and universities, and increasingly in many schools and also in businesses or other organizations. A VLE typically has the following features:

- password protected
- provides access to learning resources, including multimedia
- provides access to documentation, e.g. handbooks and other guides
- provides access to online tests
- provides a means for students to submit assignments
- provides communication tools:
  — asynchronous tools such as discussion groups, e-mail, blogging tool
  — synchronous tools such as a chat or meeting room
- provides collaborative work tools, e.g. wikis
- provides links to other resources, e.g. digitized reading lists
- provides links to other resources on the internet, e.g. company websites, professional bodies.

Advantages of VLEs:

- They are commonly available.
- They are normally paid for by the parent organization rather than the library or information service.

- They provide a standard set of tools which are normally easy to use.
- They are particularly useful as a means of supporting distance learners or blended learning.

Disadvantages of VLEs:

- They may be 'owned' by another part of the organization and the library or information worker may have little say in how they are organized. In educational institutions they are often organized into module or course sites, which may not suit the library or information service's practices.
- They normally require password access, and this may put off some users.
- It may not be possible to personalize them, leading to a rather dull learning environment.
- There may be limits to the size of files which can be uploaded, e.g. multimedia resources.

How can VLEs be used in training?

- They provide a means for disseminating learning resources either before or after a training event.
- They provide a means for communicating with learners, e.g. through the discussion board.
- It is possible to establish 'guest speakers' through the chat or meeting room function.
- Collaborative working can be set up, involving use of the discussion board, chat or meeting room, and/or wiki.

Case study 4.7 Using a VLE for teaching referencing skills

Nihal was responsible for teaching referencing skills within the science faculty of a university. She approached this by providing all students with an introductory lecture, which included a video clip of a student talking about his experience of failing a taught module owing to accidentally plagiarizing a website by failing to reference it accurately. Her supporting VLE site included: the PowerPoint presentation from her lecture; four video clips; an online test; guidance about referencing. Two weeks prior to the students' first assessed assignment, Nihal e-mailed them via the VLE and advised them to double-check their references, using her guidance materials, and also offered a number of drop-in sessions in the library. She found that about 60% of the students used her VLE site and about a dozen always called in to her drop-in session. Anecdotally, academic staff reported that they were very pleased with the quality of the students' referencing skills.

Case study 4.8 A LibGuides presence in a Blackboard environment

Bowen (2012) describes and evaluates the use of research guides generated via special software (LibGuides) and embedded into the Blackboard VLE. The study demonstrates how students value having easy access to library guides embedded within their course material and how they used it before they searched the internet. The purpose of the project was twofold: to place library resources in the same virtual space where students were working on their coursework; and to offer instruction on how to use these resources. The author points out that this approach to delivering library resources involves co-ordination among librarians, tutors and information technology staff.

Virtual talks

The internet provides access to an extensive range of online talks and presentations, e.g. through sites such as YouTube. One extremely useful site is the 'TED' site at www.ted.com/talks. The site provides access to tens of thousands of talks in a wide range of languages. It provides excellent training resources. For example, a search on the term 'librarian' came up with 260 results. However, it is possible to spend a lot of time looking for relevant and appropriate resources.

Alternatively, you can make your own audio recording or video (see Audio files, Podcasts and Videos).

Virtual visitor

Tools such as Skype or videoconferencing enable guest speakers to be welcomed to training events. A virtual visitor, timed to give a brief presentation as part of a training course, can provide a shift in focus and change of pace. It is important to thoroughly test the technology beforehand, as it is very frustrating to have a group waiting to observe and discuss an issue with a virtual visitor, but for the technology to fail.

Case study 4.9 Information wizard

A group of students were attending an evening class and were working on a specific assignment which required access to and the use of a range of information resources. The tutor librarian was unable to provide them with face-to-face support but promised to visit the course's online site at regular intervals. He used a discussion group on the site and it became a lively virtual space and he was given the nickname 'The Information Wizard'. Overall, he was able to work well with the group and they were full of praise for 'their wizard' in their feedback forms.

Web-based training

Many library and information services provide web-based training, e.g. through their website or the organization's VLE. Web-based training is a common means of providing individuals with self-study materials, which incorporate a range of learning resources and activities including:

- general guidance to help people work through relevant learning materials and activities
- items that can be downloaded, e.g. handouts and guides
- multimedia resources, e.g. videos or audio recordings
- quizzes and self-assessment tools
- frequently asked questions (and their answers)
- opportunities to post an online question or comment
- opportunities to contact a librarian for further assistance.

The advantages of web-based training are that the learners are able to:

- learn at their own pace
- use it in their own time or as part of a class-based activity
- move back and forth through the tutorial and repeat sections as necessary.

Disadvantages include:

- the time and cost involved in developing the tutorial
- the challenge of providing a web-based tutorial which looks professional
- maintaining and updating the tutorial
- web-based tutorials don't suit everyone's learning style.

Numerous examples of web-based training are available on the internet, and they include:

- LION: Library Information literacy Online Network, http://blip.tv/LIONTV
- Academic Integrity at the University of Auckland, http://flexiblelearning.auckland.ac.nz/academic_integrity/52.html
- IL information literacy website – provides links to tutorials from around the world, www.informationliteracy.org.uk.

Germek (2011), writing in the context of an American university library, states:

> Developing a successful online tutorial, however, is time- and labour-intensive, as librarians may require skills in a variety of areas, such as storyboarding, graphics development, knowledge of HTML, and Sharable Content Object Reference Model (SCORM), Java, Flash and strong writing talents to produce clear and effective learning objectives matched to measurable outcomes. Once basic tutorial development has been achieved, however, librarians can reduce their teaching loads

associated with repetitive basic library instruction, enhance library web presence, foster successful distance learning platforms, and potentially capture and report valuable assessment data.

(Germek, 2011, 90–1)

A wide range of tools are available for the development of web-based training and a good starting-point is your parent organization's own IT department as this may already have access to existing systems, and also expertise which individual librarians can tap into. Many VLEs, such as Blackboard, provide tools which can be used to develop online training programmes. Alternatively, other tools can be used to create online tutorials. Germek (2011) describes the use of Adobe Captivate and Adobe Connect to produce online library tutorials that capture assessment and usage data. His research indicated that these tools enabled librarians to update and correct tutorials easily; score assessments instantaneously; and easily customize the tutorials for students from different disciplines.

Example 4.7 Skills in accessing, finding and reviewing information (Safari)

The Open University provides a free online web-based training course called Skills in Accessing, Finding & Reviewing Information (Safari), which is available at www.open. ac.uk/safari. The course is divided into seven sections:

1 Understanding information
2 Unpacking information
3 Planning a search
4 Searching for information
5 Evaluating information
6 Organizing information
7 Where do I go from here?

This is an interesting course and it demonstrates features such as: clear guidance, 'clean' looking pages with space, and interactivity. It includes activities, e.g. section 5 has an activity that involves evaluating three different articles and completing a table (which can be printed off).
    The Open University site also provides access to additional learning resources.[6]

Example 4.8 JISC Netskills

JISC Netskills has been in existence since 1995 and provides a wide range of web-based training resources and materials (see www.netskills.ac.uk). These include face-to-face workshops and online delivery and training materials. It provides 'Share', which is a repository of Netskills content available for individual use. This material is well worth exploring, e.g. the section on 'Communication and collaboration' covers the following topics in a clear and accessible manner:

- blogging
- writing for the web
- social media
- podcasting
- microblogging
- collaborative writing.

Example 4.9 Skills@Library, University of Leeds Library
The University of Leeds Library website has a section called Skills@Library (http://library.leeds.ac.uk/skills), which provides support for students, staff and researchers in the following areas:

- exams
- finding information
- group work
- improve your maths
- learning in a digital age
- listening and interpersonal skills
- plagiarism
- presentation skills
- reading skills
- referencing
- time management
- writing skills.

The section on plagiarism includes the following resources:

- an interactive presentation (which includes voice-over speech and also access to a script)
- a plagiarism quiz
- a number of activities
- a plagiarism awareness guide
- a link to the Students' Union, Academic Advice, cheating and plagiarism page.

Overall, this website provides an impressive array of student-friendly resources that can be used independently or linked into sessions delivered by library staff or academics.

Web-based tutorials are also considered in Chapter 7.

Web conferencing
The most popular form of web conferencing is probably Skype, a free, internet-based service which provides a range of facilities including phone calls, video

calls, group video calls, screen sharing and instant messaging. It is accessible via smartphones, laptops, tablets and PC computers. In terms of training, Skype can be used for a range of activities, including:

- individual coaching sessions
- group discussions
- guest speakers
- presentations.

Case study 4.10 Information literacy instruction for satellite university students

Nicholson and Eva (2011) describe and evaluate the use of Skype to provide information literacy instruction for students based on satellite campuses. They used Skype to deliver live presentations, which were projected onto a classroom screen, to students. The instruction included screen sharing (PowerPoint presentation and also live demonstrations) and exercises. A librarian was present in the room to provide additional support. One of the disadvantages of this approach was the difficulty of gauging students' responses from their body language. It was impossible to screen share and have a camera on the classroom at the same time. At one stage the screen-sharing system stopped working.

Example 4.10 Supporting library users in the construction industry

Nathan provides a library and information service in a private company which has more than 15 sites across the UK. He regularly uses Skype as a means to introduce himself to new staff; provide verbal feedback on information searches (which he follows up with an e-mail); and to give guidance on relevant information resources. The company has a culture of using Skype and Nathan finds it a valuable tool for keeping in touch with his customers.

Webinars

The term 'webinar' is used to describe web conferencing where groups of individuals come together for an event. There are many different tools available that enable webinars, e.g. Workcast (www.workcast.co.uk) and Webex (www.webex.com), and typically they provide the following types of facilities:

- slide-show presentations with audience access to speaker
- live or streaming video
- real-time audio communication via headphones and speakers
- web tours
- whiteboards (and participants may annotate them)
- text chat (in public or private)
- polls and surveys
- screen sharing/desktop sharing/application sharing.

Webinars can be used in training to provide live and/or recorded sessions as follows:

- to support professional development (for example, see www.nefin2.blogspot.co.uk and also www.techsoupforlibraries.org/events)
- for professional conferences. Some examples include:
  — International Federation of Library Associations (IFLA), www.ifla.org, which provides regular webinars on topical subjects
  — Association for Library Services to Children (ALSC), which provides monthly webinars, www.ala.org/alsc/edcareers/profdevelopment/alscweb/webinars
  — Canadian Association of Law Libraries, www.callacbd.ca/en/content/home
  — Art Libraries Society of North America (ARLIS), www.arlisna.org/webinars/index.html
- for staff development, e.g. Texas State Library and Archives Commission, www.tsl.state.tx.us/id/workshops/webinars
- to support users of a particular product, e.g. RefWorks, www.refworks.com/training/ and OCLC, www.oclc.org/uk/en/dewey/news/conferences/default.htm
- to support database users, e.g. www.apa.org/pubs/databases/training provides access to webinars on the use of PsychInfo
- by specialist organizations, e.g. National Literacy Trust, www.literacytrust.org.uk/resources.

TIP FOR TRAINERS

As a follow-up to a short course, you could organize a webinar. This would provide a means of updating colleagues and give an opportunity for discussions and/or question-and-answer sessions after course participants have had the opportunity to practise their learning from your workshop in their own workplace.

Web portals

Many institutional libraries and information services host a web portal, which enables them to bring together a wide range of web and media resources and tools. This section is focused on personal web portals.

Increasingly, individuals subscribe to a wide range of Web 2.0 tools and this has led to the development of tools such as My Yahoo!, iGoogle, Pageflakes and Netvibes, which enable the development of a personal web portal bringing together information from diverse sources such as social networking tools, books, YouTube, Second Life, RSS feeds, etc.[7]

Individual trainers who do not have access to an institutional portal may wish to develop their own site in order to bring together a diverse range of Web 2.0

tools and facilities either for promotion or to support their customers.

Wikis

The most famous wiki is Wikipedia. Essentially, wikis are a means of collaborative writing, as individuals can edit the web pages of a wiki. The word 'wiki' comes from a Hawaiian word meaning 'fast' or 'quick'. Basically, a wiki provides a tool which enables a group of people to make contributions by adding new information, editing existing information or establishing hyperlinks between wiki pages and with resources beyond the wiki. Essentially, wikis are 'work in progress' and in a constant state of development and change. There are a number of different kinds of wiki, including: public wikis; librarian, student or lecturer wikis, provided as part of a VLE; and corporate wikis.

Advantages of wikis:

- They are easy to use.
- They are a commonly used tool (many people have used Wikipedia).
- They are a useful tool for enabling a group of people to develop a report or other document.
- They provide a means for individuals to work together when they are separated by geography and/or time.

Disadvantages of wikis:

- Without an editor, a wiki may present inaccurate or out-of-date information.
- Without an editor, there may be spelling or grammatical errors in the wiki.
- If a number of different people are contributing to a wiki, then there may be differences in the style and tone of entries.

How can wikis be used in training?

1 Wikis are very useful for collaborative projects which encourage teamworking or writing skills.
2 A group could be asked to develop a series of training resources.
3 A group could be asked to research a topic and then develop a wiki showcasing key ideas, images and links to other resources.
4 A wiki could be established that focuses on a specific resource, e.g. a database, and individuals could be asked to contribute their own tips and comments about it.
5 Wikipedia is a useful tool for demonstrating an information resource which provides both accurate and inaccurate information.

Case study 4.11 Using a wiki for sharing resources

Nick was a trainer working in a university staff development department. His area of responsibility included library training and he established a wiki to enable all the academic librarians who carried out training to share resources, links and ideas. Nick 'owned' the site and helped to ensure that it was well maintained. Twice a year he organized a lunchtime meeting where all the 'wiki workers' came together and shared ideas for future development and activities. He found that these face-to-face meetings helped to reinvigorate and remotivate the group.

Summary

Technology-enhanced learning has become an everyday reality for library and information workers involved in training and development. This is a constantly changing and developing field. It is possible for individual trainers to enhance their training events using fairly basic technologies, e.g. e-mail, podcasts and blogs. Alternatively, whole programmes and events can be developed using more sophisticated technologies.

Notes

1 http://puzzlemaker.discoveryeducation.com/choosepuzzle.
2 http://jiscdesignstudio.pbworks.com.
3 http://jiscdesignstudio.pbworks.com.
4 http:// skillsforlearning.leedsmet.ac.uk.
5 www.thedaringlibrarian.com/2012/05/qr-code-quest-scavenger-hunt-part-deux.html.
6 http://openlearn.open.ac.uk/course/category.php?id=12.
7 A good example of a personal portal is
   www.netvibes.com/sheilawebber#Sheila's_Web_2.0_stuff.

References and additional resources

Ally, M. and Needham, G. (eds) (2010) *M-Libraries 2: a virtual library in everyone's pocket*, Facet Publishing.

Ally, M. and Needham, G. (eds) (2012) *M-Libraries 3: transforming libraries with mobile technology*, Facet Publishing.

Bowen, A. (2012) A LibGuide Presence in a Blackboard Environment, *Reference Services Review*, **40** (3), 449–68.

Bradley, P. (2007) *How to Use Web 2.0 in Your Library*, Facet Publishing. Second edition to be published 2014.

Bush, D. A. (2010) Evaluation of an Audience Response System in Library Orientation for Engineering Students, *Issues in Science and Technology Librarianship*, www.istl.org/10-winter/article1.html [accessed on 14/08/2012].

Cann, A., Dimitriou, K. and Hooley, T. (2011) *Social Media: a guide for researchers*, www.rin.ac.uk/our-work/communicating-and-disseminatingresearch/social-media-guide-researchers [accessed on 13 January 2012].

Clark, J. A. (2012) *Building Mobile Library Applications*, Facet Publishing.

Cottrell, S. and Morris, N. (2012) *Study Skills Connected. Using technology to support your studies*, Palgrave.

Croft, K., Maxwell, J. and Scopes, M. (2011) A Sound Education: using podcasts to develop study skills, *SCONUL Focus* **51**, 42–5.

Germek, G. (2011) Empowering Library eLearning: capturing assessment and reporting with ease, efficiency and effectiveness, *Reference Services Review*, **40** (1), 90–102.

Godwin, P. and Parker, J. (2008) *Information Literacy Meets Library* 2.0, Facet Publishing.

Godwin, P. and Parker, J. (2012) *Information Literacy beyond Library* 2.0, Facet Publishing.

Goldsmith, F. (2012) *Apps for Librarian Productivity*, www.infoblog.infopeople.org/2012/ [accessed on 1 September 2012].

Houghton-Jan, S. (2010) *Technology Training in Libraries*, Facet Publishing.

Jones, N., Morgan, N., Nicholas, S. and Swain, E. (2011) Movie Magic: the thrill of Hollywood enhances information literacy teaching at Cardiff, *SCONUL Focus*, **51**, 45–9.

Junco, R., Heiberfer, G. and Loken, E. (2011) The Effect of Twitter on College Student Engagement and Grades, *Journal of Computer Assisted Learning*, **27**, 119–32.

Kanesho, K. N., Emmett, T. W., London, S. K., Ralston, R. K., Richwine, M. W., Skopelja, E. N., Brahmi, F. A. and Whipple, E. (2008) Use of an Audience Response System in an Evidence-based Mini-curriculum, *Medical Reference Services Quarterly*, **27** (3), 284–301.

MacDonald, J. and Creanor, L. (2010) *Learning with Online and Mobile Technologies: a student survival guide*, Gower.

Measday, B. (2006) Show Me What You Mean! Interactive whiteboards in the library, *Connections*, **56**, www2.curriculum.edu.au/scis/connections/ [accessed on 3 September 2012].

Mestre, L. S. (2012) Student Preference for Tutorial Design: a usability study, *Reference Services Review*, **40** (2), 258–76.

Nicholson, H. and Eva, N. (2011) Information Literacy Instruction for Satellite University Students, *Reference Services Review*, **39** (3), 497–513.

Notess, G. (2012) *Screencasting for Libraries*, Facet Publishing.

Peltier-Davis, C. A. (2012) *The Cybrarian's Web. An A–Z guide to 101 free Web 2.0 tools and other resources*, Plexus.

Robinson, T. S. C. (2010) *Library Videos and Webcasts*, Facet Publishing.

Salmon, G. (2002) *E-tivities: the key to active online learning*, Kogan Page.

Salmon, G., Edirisingha, P., Mobbs, M., Mobbs, R. and Dennett, C. (2008) *How to Create Podcasts for Education*, Open University Press.

Tian, S. W., Yu, A. Y., Vogel, D. and Kwok, R. C. W. (2011) The Impact of Online

Social Networking on Learning, *International Journal of Networking and Virtual Organisations*, 8, 264–80.

Whitton, N. and Moseley, A. (eds) (2012) *Using Games to Enhance Learning and Teaching*, Routledge.

5

Making it happen

Introduction

This chapter is concerned with the activities that need to take place in order to ensure that training events are well designed and evaluated, and also marketed and promoted. The starting-point for thinking about any training event is the learners and their needs, and this is explored under the headings: library and information users and their needs; supporting learners with disabilities; and working with international students.

This is followed by a detailed section on designing training events. Why spend time designing learning and teaching activities? There are a number of reasons for taking the time to work out the detail of your training programme and these include:

- giving yourself confidence
- focusing your thinking on the learners
- preparation of learning materials
- meeting problems with contingency plans
- thinking through the whole event
- reduced likelihood of making basic errors
- looking professional.

The section covers basic design principles and explores different approaches to structuring face-to-face training events. (E-learning and blended learning programmes will be considered in Chapter 7.) The design of a training event involves thinking about evaluation and incorporating this into the structure of the event. Frequently, evaluation is considered at the end of books on training, but if it is to be properly designed, then it needs to be considered at the same time as the design process. The Kirkpatrick (1994) model is used to describe different levels of and approaches to training evaluation.

The last section in this chapter focuses on marketing and promoting training events. It describes common approaches to ensuring that the appropriate participants attend training events and ends with a series of case studies which explore current practice.

Example 5.1 Planning and designing training events

Harding (2012) writes:

> *To be effective, training courses demand meticulous and lengthy planning. They must be geared to the needs of the delegates, and to organisational needs. I spend a lot of time in preliminary discussions about these issues with training providers. Sometimes they change what they have initially asked for as a result, realising that an amended focus or methodology is likely to be more successful. I use the experience I have built up over many years as a trainer to plan course programmes, content and training strategies. In terms of content, this is particularly important when I am planning a course that is for delegates from a variety of organisations, as I cannot make use of local knowledge. I always provide draft proposals to clients, and make changes in the light of their feedback. Timings for courses have to be thought through carefully. The most important planning task, as I see it, is working out ways to help people develop their knowledge, skills and confidence without lecturing from the front, as this rarely works. Devising the right questions to ask so as to motivate discussion and learning is crucial.*

Thinking about participants

Library and information users and their needs

Library and information users are a diverse group, as indicated by their ages, cultural backgrounds, emotional intelligence, employment experiences, ethnic backgrounds, faiths, financial situations, genders, information technology skills, languages, learning styles, life experiences, literacy and numeracy, nationalities, previous educational experiences or special needs. Trainers will work with diverse groups, and a basic rule of training is to be inclusive and to plan, design and deliver the training event so that all participants achieve the learning outcomes and feel comfortable and welcomed to the group.

TIP FOR TRAINERS

Before you plan your training course, think about the participants. Who is likely to come to your course? How could you find out more about your participants? Is there anything about them that you need to take into account in your training design and delivery?

When working with diverse groups it is important to:

- avoid stereotypes in examples and case studies
- use examples that are inclusive

- ensure that images are representative of wider society
- use pair and small-group work to help everyone to engage with the training event
- ask individuals who are quiet for their opinions and thoughts
- challenge discriminatory language or behaviours
- think about what you say and do – what will be its impact on the whole group?

If you are concerned that you are not making reasonable adjustments to meet the needs of individuals, then ask them (perhaps during a refreshment break) whether or not you are supporting their learning needs.

Similarly, when working with diverse groups it is important to *avoid*:

- using stereotypes in your examples or images
- letting some individuals dominate the training event, and so marginalizing other people
- asking individuals to represent a group, e.g. 'Bushra, as a Muslim, what types of display do you think we should organize?'
- ignoring any unacceptable comments or statements. If this happens, then it is best to tackle them in an appropriate manner.

Supporting learners with disabilities

In the UK, the Equality Act 2010 provides a legal context for supporting individuals with disabilities. Library and information workers in the education sector (schools, colleges and universities) and other public sector organizations are likely to have help from specialist staff or departments in supporting individuals with disabilities. In the private sector this support may come from a specialist within the human resources department. This means that individual trainers are provided with information about the 'reasonable adjustments' that need to take place in order to support an individual. Alternatively, the trainer needs to meet with or at least to discuss with the learner and identify the required adjustment(s).

This adjustment is often very simple to achieve and may require:

- the production and dissemination of handouts and training guides in advance of the training event. These may be in electronic format
- the use of a particular typeface or paper colour in handouts and training guides
- the use of a minimum font size in presentations, e.g. 30 point Arial or Verdana
- the provision of a transcript of a video (for individuals with a hearing impairment)

- allowing the learner to make an audio recording of the training event
- the use of a microphone by the trainer to help everyone to hear the training event
- the use of specialist technology in the training event by the individual with the disability
- the presence of a support worker or carer.

In terms of delivering the training session, the trainer needs to be careful to:

- learn how to make sure that everyone can hear everything that is said in the teaching event by:
  — never speaking with their back to the group
  — repeating the questions or comments of group members so that everyone can hear them
  — ensuring that only one person speaks at a time
  — banning private conversations
- learn how to verbalize visual information:
  — in spoken language, e.g. rather than using phrases such as 'over there', by saying 'by the door'
  — by developing explanations for diagrams or images on PowerPoint presentations
- learn how to manage the timings of activities so that everyone has time to engage with them. This may mean providing case studies in advance for some individuals with special needs
- provide pauses for reflection, questions and clarification
- provide summaries of main points.

Supporting the needs of learners with disabilities is actually good training practice and will result in all participants benefiting from the training event. Trainers can develop their knowledge of and experience in working with people with disabilities by making use of the following resources:

- The training and guidance on supporting individuals with disabilities which may be organized and provided by the human resources department or a specialist unit within the organization. It is important for trainers to be up to date on this topic and to understand the implications of the relevant legislation – in the UK, it is the Equality Act 2010.
- The website www.w3.org, which provides help and guidance on providing accessible websites. A search of this website shows that it provides guidance on a wide range of topics. For example, under 'How to make presentations accessible to all' it covers the following topics:
  — basics (organizers and speakers)

— benefits (organizers and speakers)
— planning the event (organizers)
— providing accessible materials and media (organizers and speakers)
— planning your session (speakers)
— preparing slides and projected material (speakers)
— during the presentation (speakers)
— for more information (speakers)
— terminology (appendix).

• Numerous websites which provide access to useful information. For example the Open University, which was a pioneering organization for supporting students with disabilities, has a very useful website at www.open.ac.uk/disability/. JISC (the Joint Information Systems Committee) champions the use of digital technology in higher education, and this includes supporting projects to help staff and students with disabilities (see www.jisc.ac.uk).
• Specialist organizations that provide support for people with disabilities often host extremely helpful websites, e.g. www.rnib.org.uk.
• Ask for feedback from people with disabilities who attend your training sessions – they will be able to let you know what helped or constrained their learning experiences.

Case study 5.1 Supporting delegates with additional needs

Jane, a trainer in a law company, was informed that a new colleague, Anne, who had a hearing impairment, would be attending her next training session. Throughout the session, she made sure that she always spoke clearly and faced the group. Her handouts covered all technical terms. When individuals asked questions or made comments, she repeated them to make sure that everyone heard what was being said. During the session, a workman began drilling in the next room. It was very loud and made it hard for everyone to hear the discussions. Jane went and asked him to come back and complete his work later on. Feedback from Anne indicated that she found the session very helpful. When Jane reflected on the experience she realized that supporting Anne's needs had actually improved the course for everyone.

Supporting international students

Many library and information workers in colleges and universities work with international students. As with any group, international students are extremely diverse, and students from the same country are equally diverse. According to Montgomery (2010), there are some common stereotypes about international students in the UK, and her research demonstrates and debunks these myths, as illustrated in Table 5.1.

Frequently, the first contact that library and information workers have with international students is at induction and orientation events. This is also the

Table 5.1 Characteristics of international students	
Common stereotype	Findings from Montgomery's research
Slow learners Have poor English Come from a country with a deficient education system Willing to cheat the system Stick with people from their own country Likely to be in trouble with the Border Agency Don't follow our rules and regulations	Curious High achievers Hard working Highly motivated Focused on studies Understand benefits of higher education Want to learn about UK culture and make friends

period when those students who have recently arrived in the country are experiencing culture shock, which means that it is not a good time for them to learn about the intricacies of libraries, database searching, referencing or plagiarism. It is sensible to restrict these induction or orientation sessions to presenting a few key points and signposting the students to future events.

International students are likely to have very varied previous academic library experiences and this may mean that some international doctoral students have little experience of using a library and academic databases. Others will have used some of the most advanced libraries and research collections in the world. In addition, international students will have very varied previous learning experiences: some of them will have all the skills required to carry out independent academic work; and others will have come from a didactic background where they were used to 'spoon feeding' and following detailed guidance and advice from their teachers and tutors.

Similarly, international students will have varied English-language skills. The English language, both spoken and written, of some students will be impeccable. Other students will find that they need to adapt to the accents and rhythms experienced in everyday academic life, but once they adjust to local or regional accents then they have no English-language issues. In contrast, some students may struggle with English, and so they may find their library (and other) training sessions challenging.

In terms of helping to support international students during training sessions, it is worthwhile using the following guidelines:

- Provide handouts in advance.
- Consider recording your sessions so that students can listen to/view them again.
- Provide a glossary of terms.
- Include practical work with feedback.
- Provide examples of 'good work'.
- Use international examples.
- Accept native-tongue discussions.

TIP FOR TRAINERS

When working with international students it is helpful to:

- provide clear guidance throughout the session, e.g. 'We are going to do three activities, the first one is.....'
- avoid culture-specific figures of speech
- keep your language neutral and be careful about using humour
- let students know that you have an interest in their culture
- make sure everyone can hear and understand contributions from all students.

There are many resources on working with international students. Useful starting-points include:

- Senior, K., Bent, M. et al. (2008) *Guidelines for Supporting International Students in the Library*
- Montgomery, C. (2010) *Understanding the International Student Experience*
- specialist training courses
- helpful websites provided by some publishers, e.g. www.palgrave.com/skills4study/
- advice and guidance provided by many colleges and universities via short courses, guidance materials and their websites.

Design principles

The starting-point for designing a training event is to spend some time thinking about and/or researching your participants and answering questions such as:

- Who is my audience?
- What is their background and experience?
- What are they likely to expect from the session?
- What will they be doing immediately before and after the training session?

Once you have answered these questions, then you can begin to think about the purpose or aim of the session and the learning outcomes.

Working out a clear aim or overall purpose of the training event will help to focus the design process. It needs to be verbalized in the form of a statement of intent, e.g.:

- The aim of the course is to enable staff to use the self-service issue system.
- The purpose of the workshop is to introduce EndNote.
- The aim of this presentation is to introduce the information service to new staff.

Once you have defined the aim, then it is important to work out the learning outcomes which specify what someone will learn as a result of the training event. Sometimes they are called 'intended learning outcomes', in recognition that individuals may learn something not anticipated by the trainer. Learning outcomes are helpful in marketing a training event because they indicate to potential participants the benefits (in terms of specific learning outcomes) that they will achieve if they attend the event. They are often used at the start of a session as a means of reminding participants of the session's focus.

Bloom's Taxonomy of Learning (introduced in Chapter 2) provides guidance on the type of language used in learning outcomes. This is illustrated in Table 5.2. It is important that the trainer is able to assess whether or not the learners have achieved the stated learning outcomes by the end of the session. Effective learning outcomes will be:

- clear and concise
- readable
- assessable.

Table 5.2 *Using Bloom's taxonomy to write learning outcomes*		
Levels of cognition	Language used in writing learning outcomes	Example learning outcomes As a result of participating in this training event, delegates will be able to:
1 Remembering	Remember, list, define, describe	List the key features of the Science Library
2 Understanding	Explain, summarize, rephrase	Explain why referencing is important in writing scientific papers
3 Application	Use in new or different situations, implement	Use Boolean logic in searching for a particular chemistry topic
4 Analysis	Compare, organize, deconstruct	Compare and contrast two chemical information sources
5 Evaluation	Judge, set and use criteria to evaluate, prioritize	Evaluate the relevance of a particular scientific paper with respect to an area under investigation
6 Creation	Design, build, construct, produce	Write an evidence-based literature review

The following are examples of learning outcomes:

- By the end of the training event, delegates will be able to search using Boolean logic.
- By the end of the training event, students will be able to list the main information sources in their subject area.
- By the end of the training event, delegates will be able to find the key links on the library website.

These three examples all use everyday language (search, list, find) to describe what people will be able to do as a result of the training session. It will also be possible to assess individuals' learning as a result of the session, e.g. by asking them to search using Boolean logic, list the main information sources in their subject area or find the key links on the library website. These three examples are all at Level 1 of Bloom's taxonomy.

TIP FOR TRAINERS

Check your draft learning outcomes against the different levels in Bloom's taxonomy. Are they written at the appropriate level?

Ask a colleague to give you feedback on your draft aim and learning outcomes for a training event. This will help you to produce carefully worded and meaningful statements. ▪

Example 5.2 Library training for users with special needsr

Hegarty (2012) describes the process of developing a training course for people with special needs and has produced a series of learning outcomes as follows:

By the end of the library training sessions, students will be able to:

- *use their college cards to enter through the library access gates*
- *behave appropriately in the library and ask library staff for assistance as required*
- *browse the library shelves for books of interest*
- *use their college cards to borrow books*
- *return library books on time so as to avoid fines.*

These sample learning outcomes are extremely easy to understand, and also to assess.

Designing face-to-face sessions

There are a number of different ways of designing the structure of a training session. Basically, every session needs to have a clear and logical structure. The simplest structure involves three parts, as shown in Figure 5.1.

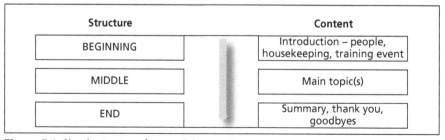

Structure	Content
BEGINNING	Introduction – people, housekeeping, training event
MIDDLE	Main topic(s)
END	Summary, thank you, goodbyes

Figure 5.1 *Simple structure for a training session*

However, this is over-simplistic and most people want to know how to structure and organize their sessions in more detail. The Honey and Mumford model of learning styles (see Chapter 2) provides some insights into the design of training sessions, sometimes called the 4MAT approach (see McCarthy, 2012), and this is summarized in Table 5.3. This is the approach that I have used in my own training practice and it seems to work.

Table 5.3 *Linking Honey and Mumford learning styles with the design of a training session*

Stage in the training event	Question answered	Learning style
Rationale and benefits of the session	Why?	Reflector
Description of the topic	What?	Theorist
Activity – practical hands-on or other activity	How?	Activist
Question time	What if?	Pragmatist

The 4MAT approach needs to be enhanced through the addition of introductions and time to summarize and close the session. This is illustrated in Figure 5.2.

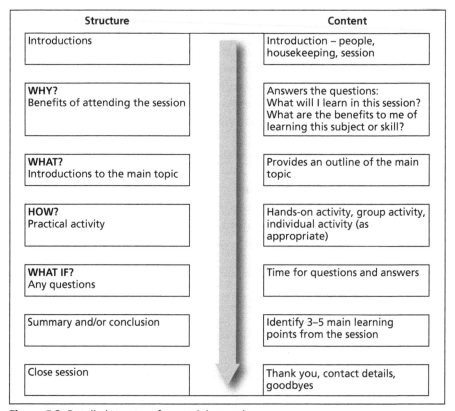

Figure 5.2 *Detailed structure for a training session*

The benefits of using this structure are:

- Introductions – allow individuals to settle down and get ready to learn
- 4MAT structure:
  — Benefits of attending – helps to convince individuals that they will benefit from engaging with the session. Examples could include: saving time; finding up-to-date materials to help with doing a job/assignments; prevention of accidental plagiarism. This is equivalent to the WHY in the Honey and Mumford learning styles model and meets the learning style preference of reflectors.
  — Introduction to the main topic – WHAT. This meets the learning style preference of theorists.
  — Practical activity – HOW. This meets the learning style preference of activists.
  — Any questions – WHAT IF. This meets the learning style preference of pragmatists.
- Summary and/or conclusion helps to remind individuals of what they have gained from the session.
- Closing the session in a professional manner helps everyone to know that it has ended and to move on to the next activity in their diary.

Impact of learning style preferences on training styles

Apparently, individual trainers are more likely to use learning and teaching methods that they themselves prefer in their training sessions. To use an over-simplified example, this means that someone whose preference is an auditory learning style will spend more time using an auditory teaching style, e.g. talking and encouraging talking within the group, rather than using visual or kinaesthetic methods.

In terms of the design of a training session, the Honey and Mumford model (see Tables 5.5 and 5.6) suggests that different styles are linked to different stages of a training session. In terms of a trainer's using their own learning style preferences, this could mean that they spend more time on the learning and teaching method that suits their own style, rather than providing a well balanced training session. This is illustrated in Table 5.4 with three examples of different training sessions:

A. a well balanced session
B. a session designed by someone with a theorist learning style, which over-emphasizes the description of the main topic
C. a session designed by someone with an activist learning style, which over-emphasizes the activity stage.

Table 5.4 *Example training event designs*

Stage in the training event	Question answered	Learning style	Time allowance
A. One-hour session introducing referencing – well-balanced session			
Rationale and benefits of the session	Why?	Reflector	5 minutes
Description of the topic	What?	Theorist	15 minutes
Activity – practical hands-on or other activity	How?	Activist	30 minutes
Question time	What if?	Pragmatist	10 minutes
B. One-hour session introducing referencing – designed by someone with a strong theorist learning style			
Rationale and benefits of the session	Why?	Reflector	5 minutes
Description of the topic	What?	Theorist	45 minutes
Activity – practical hands-on or other activity	How?	Activist	5 minutes
Question time	What if?	Pragmatist	5 minutes
C. One-hour session introducing referencing – designed by someone with a strong activist learning style			
Rationale and benefits of the session	Why?	Reflector	1 minute
Description of the topic	What?	Theorist	5 minutes
Activity – practical hands-on or other activity	How?	Activist	50 minutes
Question time	What if?	Pragmatist	4 minutes

This is an over-simplified example and, in reality, a trainer needs to take many factors into account when designing a session. However, knowledge of learning styles does enable us to develop well balanced sessions which support a range of learning styles.

Managing session timings

Librarians and information workers new to training often ask more experienced trainers how to manage timings. The question is a difficult one to answer. There is no hard and fast rule, and to a certain extent it depends on the audience, the topic and the trainer. Table 5.5 gives two worked examples of timings: one for a one-hour session and one for a two-hour session. The same approach and structures can be used for planning a half-day or one-day training session. Table 5.6 provides these two worked examples.

Table 5.5 *Indicative timing of sessions*

One-hour session		Two-hour session	
5 minutes	Introductions	5 minutes	Introductions
2 minutes	Benefits of attending the session	5 minutes	Benefits of attending the session
10 minutes	Introduction to the main topic	30 minutes	Introduction to the main topic
30 minutes	Practical activity	60 minutes	Practical activity
10 minutes	Any questions	10 minutes	Any questions
2 minutes	Summary and/or conclusion	8 minutes	Summary and/or conclusion
1 minute	Close session	2 minutes	Close session

Table 5.6 *Planning a longer training session*			
Half-day session		**Whole-day session**	
10 minutes	Introductions	5 minutes	Introductions
5 minutes	Benefits of attending the session	5 minutes	Benefits of attending the session
10 minutes	Introduction to Topic 1	10 minutes	Introduction to Topic 1
30 minutes	Practical activity	30 minutes	Practical activity
10 minutes	Any questions – Topic 1	10 minutes	Any questions – Topic 1
20 minutes	**Break**	20 minutes	**Break**
10 minutes	Introduction to Topic 2	10 minutes	Introduction to Topic 2
30 minutes	Practical activity	30 minutes	Practical activity
10 minutes	Any questions – Topic 2	10 minutes	Any questions – Topic 2
10 minutes	Summary activity	10 minutes	Summary activity – whole morning
5 minutes	Action planning	45 minutes	**Lunch**
5 minutes	Evaluation	10 minutes	Activity to help everyone focus after lunch
5 minutes	Close of session	10 minutes	Introduction to Topic 3
		30 minutes	Practical activity
		10 minutes	Any questions – Topic 3
		15 minutes	**Break**
		10 minutes	Introduction to Topic 4
		30 minutes	Practical activity
		10 minutes	Any questions – Topic 4
		15 minutes	Whole group summary activity
		10 minutes	Action planning
		5 minutes	Training session evaluation
		5 minutes	Close of session

Example 5.3 Timing and refreshments

Harding (2012) writes:

Attention levels are limited, and being a delegate on a course is harder work than is often realised. I find it crucial to break training days up, not only with plenty of variety, but also with sufficient downtime. On most of my training events, each session lasts no more than an hour and a half – many are an hour and a quarter. Each is followed by a break: 15 minutes in the morning and afternoon, with drinks and refreshments, three-quarters of an hour or an hour for lunch, depending on the time available. I am strict about getting everyone back on time at the end of each break. It is not fair on those delegates who observe the timings to be held up by less thoughtful colleagues, and can breed negativity. Lunch on site saves time, keeps delegates more focused and, very importantly, provides opportunities for informal discussion.

Sometimes library and information workers have limited opportunities to train their customers. For example, in academic libraries there is often an opportunity during induction to speak to a large and captive audience of students. Similarly, in workplace libraries there is often an opportunity to train people as part of their induction or orientation. At these times there is often a tendency to cram as much material as possible into the session, as it may be felt that another opportunity to meet with the individual or group may not arise easily. This tends to be counterproductive. Induction is not the best time for people to take in vital information, as they are still getting used to their new surroundings and orienting themselves. A few key points delivered in a clear and uncluttered manner are more likely to be remembered than an hour stuffed with detail upon detail about the library, catalogue, databases, referencing and plagiarism.

The last topic in this section is documenting the training design. It is important to produce a written record of your training plan as it provides a check of the following points:

- that the aim and learning outcomes are appropriate
- that the structure is logical
- that you have covered a range of learning styles
- that your participants are involved in a range of different learning activities
- that all of the learning outcomes are likely to be achieved during the course.

Figure 5.3 is a form for capturing the details of a training course. It enables a trainer to:

- record the aims and learning outcomes
- identify any resources required
- double-check health and safety issues when entering the training room
- include an indicative timing for each learning or teaching activity
- use the trainer and learner activity columns to check for:
  — a logical structure
  — use of a variety of training methods
  — use of a variety of learning methods
- check that each learning outcome is covered by one or more activities – using the final column, 'learning outcomes'.

Evaluation of training

The design stage of a training event includes making decisions about how it will be evaluated. Evaluation is important, as it provides vital information for both the trainer and the library and information service. The purpose of evaluation is to answer questions aimed at different audiences.

- Library and information service:
  — To what extent did the training activities support our goals, objectives and KPIs?
  — Did the training event help to improve the reputation of the service?

Course title				
Aim(s)				
Learning outcomes	1. 2. 3.			
Resources required				

Time	Topic	Trainer activity	Learner activity	Learning outcomes
Before start of event	Health and safety	Check room, etc.	n/a	

Figure 5.3 *Pro-forma for a training course plan*

— Did the training event help to promote our service?
- Trainers:
  — To what extent were the training aims and learning outcomes achieved?
  — What worked well and what could be improved?
  — How can I improve my training practice with this evaluation?
- Stakeholders and sponsors:
  — Did the training support our goal(s)?
  — Has our money been well spent?
  — Did the training event achieve its purpose?

The Kirkpatrick (1994) model is commonly used for evaluating training. It has four levels:

- reaction – what participants thought and felt about the training
- learning – what they learnt as a result of the training
- behaviour – the impact of the training on the participants' behaviour, e.g. at work or in their educational course
- impact – the effect on the library and information service, and on the parent organization.

Each level is associated with particular evaluation methods, which are outlined in Table 5.7.

Table 5.7 *Tools for evaluation*

Tool	Level of evaluation			
	Reactions	Learning	Behaviour	Impact on ILS
Software tracking tools			•	•
Online or paper-based questionnaires or reports	•	•	•	•
Team leader or manager questionnaires or reports	•	•	•	•
Online assessment activities		•	•	
Customer survey			•	•
Employer survey			•	•
Interviews	•	•	•	•
Focus group	•	•		
Performance appraisal		•	•	
Observation	•	•	•	
Team/unit performance indicators			•	•
ILS performance indicators				•

The reaction of individuals to the training event can be gauged through simple questionnaires or surveys. Typical questions to ask include:

- Did the training event meet your expectations?

- Did you achieve the learning outcomes of the course?
- What did you learn from the event?
- What did you like best about the training event?
- How could the event be improved?
- Please comment on the venue/refreshments.
- Please comment on the administration of the event.
- Would you recommend this course to a colleague? If not, please explain.

A difficulty that arises with very short training sessions is that completing a questionnaire can sometimes seem like overkill. However, feedback from participants is important and there are some simple and quick ways of collecting feedback from individuals, pairs or small groups and involving sticky notes, paper or flipcharts/whiteboards. Methods include:

- Quadrant method. Divide the flipchart paper (or whiteboard) into four sections and then ask the questions shown in Figure 5.4.
- Stop, start, continue. Race (1999) describes this method, in which the trainer gives each participant three sticky notes at the start of the session and asks them to write either stop, start or continue on each note. As they go through the training event, they can complete the sticky notes and record what they want the trainer to stop, start or continue doing. The notes can then be collected at the end of the event (or during an appropriate break).

What did you like about the training event?	What could be improved about the training event?
What did you learn from the event?	What will you do as a result of this experience?

Figure 5.4 *Quick feedback method*

Evaluating what individuals have learnt from a training event may involve a range of different activities including:

- use of diagnostic tests and end-of-training tests. These may be delivered online, on paper or as a group game.
- use of observation during the event. As a trainer, during the event you can observe whether or not participants:

- — use the technical language introduced in the event
- — use the search techniques introduced in an information skills session
- — ask questions or make comments that indicate they have learnt the required knowledge or skill.
- arranging interviews towards the end of the training event or soon after. The interviews may be used to evaluate individuals' use of technical language and their ability to describe the skills they have gained from the training event. However, this is a self-reporting process and so it may not be very accurate. It is also time consuming.

The next level of evaluation relates to finding out the impact of the training on the participants' behaviour, e.g. at work or in their educational course. This can be obtained by:

- observation in the workplace – for staff. This may involve observing:
- — use of technical language
- — practical skills.
- observation in the library or information service – for customers. This may involve observing:
- — their use of a help desk or online service
- — their use of library resources.
- interviews with participants and/or their managers and/or their tutors (in educational institutions):
- — Interviews with participants are a self-reporting process and so may not be very accurate. They are also quite time consuming.
- — Interviews with managers or tutors provide a third-person perspective, but this is a time consuming method and these people may not have the necessary knowledge to be able to give useful feedback.

The fourth and last level of evaluation involves measuring the effect of the training on the performance of the library and information service and of the parent organization. This is likely to involve the following:

- feedback from quality assurance systems, customer service surveys, other feedback mechanisms
- data from online tracking tools, e.g. use of databases, virtual learning environments, etc.

Stevenson (2012) provides a critique of the Kirkpatrick model and a detailed analysis of other approaches to evaluation in the context of health service libraries. In reality, the majority of library and information trainers appear to evaluate their training events in terms of the reaction (end-of-course questionnaires or activities) or learning (diagnostic tests and quizzes or observation). These are the two measures that are the easiest to collect and analyse. The other two measures are much more difficult to evaluate and it can sometimes appear tenuous to link a particular training event or events with changes in the performance of the library and information service. This doesn't mean that it is not worth doing, but it can be difficult!

Example 5.4 Evaluation from the perspective of an independent trainer

Harding (2012), writing about her training courses in the field of school librarianship, writes:

> I ask for evaluation at the end of every training course I give. Delegate feedback is crucial to me: it really helps me to develop my courses. I have tried a number of different evaluation methods over the years, and have experience of a wide diversity of organisational evaluation forms. Numerical systems almost invariably cause problems. Whatever the rubric says, there are always some delegates who get the numbering the wrong way round. In addition, lots of people automatically give every question the same mark, rather than thinking in any depth. Delegates' written comments often contradict their scores. I understand why training organisers use such systems, but they rarely produce genuinely valuable data. Closed questions are also not helpful: they lead inevitably to closed answers. My evaluation form now simply asks delegates to make any comments they wish about the course. The quality of responses is wonderful and truly useful to me and my clients.

Marketing and promoting training programmes

Marketing training programmes is the process of creating, communicating and delivering training programmes. It involves letting other people know about our activities so that they either get involved or support us. The process of creating training programmes involves identifying and establishing training needs (described earlier in this chapter and also in Chapter 1). This includes developing a relationship with stakeholders (relationship marketing), which itself will have an impact on whether or not stakeholders are committed to and value the training. The process of communicating about training events is the main focus of this section. The final stage in the marketing process involves delivering training programmes, and this is covered in Chapters 6 and 7.

The concept of the 'four Ps' in marketing means analysing the following:

- Product: what is on offer?
- Price: what does it cost to develop and deliver?
- Place: how and where will it be delivered – location, face-to-face/e-learning/blended learning, accessibility.
- Promotion: how will users know what is available?

The hierarchy of effects model (Clow and Baack, 2007) provides an insight into stakeholders' thinking processes about training programmes, and this is likely to involve a number of stages:

- awareness
- knowledge
- liking
- preference
- conviction
- purchase (or sign-up for the training event).

Communicating with colleagues or customers about training programmes is an activity that is likely to involve using a number of different media, including e-mail, e-bulletins, websites and social media tools such as blogs, wikis, Facebook, LinkedIn, podcasts, video clips and printed flyers and posters. These will be considered in turn.

- E-mails can be livened up by including colour and images and embedding links to video clips, e.g. from satisfied training participants.
- E-bulletins (see Chapter 8).
- Websites: technical skills are required to produce excellent websites. Some key points include: clarity of visual design, information and navigation. In addition, they need to be designed for accessibility to people with disabilities (see www.w3.org).
- Social media tools are considered in depth in Chapter 4; they may be used to communicate with selected audiences.
- Video clips can be made quickly and cheaply, e.g. using a mobile phone, and disseminated via e-mail or websites. A short (two to three minutes) video of a satisfied course participant talking about the benefits gained from the training event is a powerful promotional tool.
- Printed flyers and posters: these are a traditional medium of communication and they are relatively easy to produce and circulate.

Involving others in the promotion of a training event is a useful tactic for encouraging attendance. It may also involve obtaining the support of a range of people. For example:

- asking team leaders to recommend training events to their team members
- asking lecturers to recommend training events to their students
- asking individuals who have taken part in a training event to recommend it to others, e.g. via a reference on the website or in training materials, or through a video-clip interview.

Case study 5.2 Induction training

Alison worked as an information officer in a research association and she ran training events on information services and resources. The Human Resources department was unwilling to let her run a session as part of new staff inductions as it felt that its induction programme was already very full. However, Alison was allowed to drop in to the coffee breaks at these events. She did so and provided each new member of staff with a paper bag containing information about the library, sticky notes, a promotional pen with the library's website and phone number, plus a printout of an introductory PowerPoint presentation. The bag also included a plastic 'biscuit' with a message inviting staff to come along for an introduction to the library the following week – at which she promised to provide coffee and biscuits. This worked well. The plastic biscuits caused laughter and Alison found that new staff did visit the library – and asked for their coffee and biscuits!

Example 5.5 Attracting teenagers

Goodstein (2008) writes about attracting teenagers to engage with libraries and their activities, and she provides the following suggestions:

- Enlist teens to manage social media.
- Ask teens to redesign your website or contribute to online content.
- Don't try too hard to be cool. Be yourself and be honest.
- Know your audience.
- Stay on top of technology and know which technologies teenagers are using.
- Use text messaging and instant messaging appropriately.
- Ask them!

Case study 5.3 Marketing information literacy week

Barker-Mathews and Costello (2011, 28) describe an 'Information Literacy Week' used to raise awareness of the importance of information literacy (IL) amongst both academic staff and students at the university. Marketing involved a range of strategies:

Our marketing strategy had to attract the attention of both students and staff, and needed to stand out amongst the plethora of other campaigns on campus. The design evolved naturally from the IL website and was based around a word-cloud logo made up of key IL terms. This was all brought together through posters, computer screensavers and internal pull-up stands. We purchased external display flags and positioned them outside key buildings in order to capture the attention of students and staff as they walked about campus. We were able to promote IL week using a number of university online channels. The IL week brand was amended and tailored to suit various websites, including that of the library (naturally), the Students' Union, the university's VLE and the Student and Staff Channels. It also featured on university plasma screens, and in two issues of the student e-newsletter.

Barker-Mathews and Costello identified a number of 'lessons learnt', which are probably relevant to any library or information worker promoting learning and teaching activities:

- *Begin planning much earlier.*
- *Be clear about what the campaign is to achieve. Our next IL week may have different objectives as the IL project develops and intended learning outcomes are embedded.*
- *Expand marketing and adopt a more innovative and proactive approach.*
- *Marketing should explain clearly the importance of IL to students and why they need it – they only want to know how it will benefit them.*
- *Contact academic staff earlier in the planning process through a series of brief but engaging emails extolling the benefits of IL.*
- *Encourage collaboration with academic colleagues in the participation and delivery of events.*
- *Advise library colleagues during IL sessions to contextualise IL for students as an invaluable tool for life.*

(Barker-Mathews and Costello, 2011, 30)

This is an interesting example because, despite extensive marketing and a very successful IL week, the authors recommend additional marketing and also encouragement of greater collaboration with key stakeholders.

Example 5.6 Anne Harding writes about marketing her training programmes

Word-of-mouth recommendation is by far the most effective form of marketing, for in-house and external training. In terms of the former, potential delegates are predisposed to feel favourably about a course recommended by a colleague. A high proportion of my training comes through recommendations, or from existing clients requesting further courses. My website is vital (see www.anneharding.net). I get frequent enquiries from training organizers who have been searching the web for trainers. Previous clients often explore it to get ideas for new training areas.

These days social networking is crucial for marketing. I use my blog to talk about training that I am currently engaged in and topics likely to be of interest to practitioners working in the fields in which I offer courses. For example, I blog about children's and young people's reading, school libraries, special needs, books I am reviewing. I find Twitter and Facebook extremely useful for alerting followers to recent research and information. I know that people value finding out about issues through me.

Summary

This chapter has focused on the design of training events. The starting-point for the design process is the participants, and so it is important to learn about who is likely to come on your training events, and to design courses that are inclusive and support different types of learners. The section on design started by looking at aims and learning outcomes which are linked with Bloom's taxonomy (see Chapter 2). This was followed by an exploration of different ways of organizing and structuring training events. An important point here is that a knowledge of learning styles (see Chapter 2) can be used to inform the design process. Evaluation needs to be designed at the same stage as designing the detailed training event. The popular Kirkpatrick model provides a framework for evaluation. The chapter concluded with a section on marketing and promoting your training courses, and includes a series of case studies and examples.

References and additional materials

Barker-Mathews, S. and Costello, M. (2011) If the Library is the Heart of the University, then Information Literacy is the Brain: promoting 'Information literacy week' at Salford University, *SCONUL Focus*, **52**, 28–30.

Clow, K. E. and Baack, D. (2007) *Integrated Advertising, Promotion and Marketing Communications*, 3rd edn, Pearson Education.

Goodstein, A. (2008) What Would Madison Avenue Do? Marketing to teens, *School Library Journal*, 5 January, www.schoollibraryjournal.com/article/CA6555544.html.

Harding, A. (2012) Personal communication.

Hegarty, N. (2012) Breaking New Ground: introducing special needs students to Waterford Institute of Technology (WIT) libraries, *SCONUL Focus*, **55**, 10–11.

Kirkpatrick, D. L. (1994) *Evaluating Training Programs*, San Berrett-Koehler Publishers.

McCarthy, B. (2012) *The 4MAT Approach to Training*, www.aboutlearning.com/ [accessed on 12 August 2012].

Mires, E. (2012) Personal Communication.

Montgomery, C. (2010) *Understanding the International Student Experience*, Palgrave Macmillan.

Race, P. (ed.) (1999) *2000 Tips for Lecturers*, Kogan Page.

Senior, K., Bent, M. et al. (2008) Guidelines for Supporting International Students in the Library, SCONUL, www.sconul.ac.uk/groups/access/papers/international_students.pdf [accessed on 20 September 2012].

Stevenson, P. (2012) Evaluating Educational Interventions for Information Literacy, *Health Information and Libraries Journal*, **29** (1), (March), 81–6.

6

Delivering face-to-face training sessions

Introduction

This chapter is concerned with delivering face-to-face training sessions. It covers the following topics: getting started; managing the learning process; questions; ending the learning process. This is followed by three examples: teaching large groups; making database training interesting; and managing challenging behaviours.

Getting started

The start of a session is always important, as this sets the tone for the whole training event. A basic rule is to arrive early (if possible). This gives you time to check the room and facilities, including:

- seating arrangements
- technology
- lighting
- layout
- all learning resources and materials
- location of toilets
- emergency exits and arrangements.

It is worthwhile starting up the technology and uploading and viewing your learning resources, e.g. PowerPoint presentation. If you are using video clips or other media, then check that the system is fully working. It is very frustrating to discover halfway through a presentation that the sound on a video clip doesn't work.

TIP FOR TRAINERS

Make sure that you have everything ready and have carried out all the checks. Then position yourself in the room so that you can meet and greet everyone as they arrive for their training event.

This gives you an opportunity to introduce yourself and begin to learn everyone's (or at least, some people's) names. It also gives them a chance to 'size you up' and begin to get to know you.

When it is time to commence the training session, you need to make a clear start. This will work best if you are relaxed and well prepared. A typical start of a session will involve the following:

- Welcome everyone to the event. Greet people and make eye contact. Start off with positive phrases: 'Welcome to this training event. I am really pleased to be here and I hope that we all have a very successful time together.'
- Start enthusiastically and with energy. This is important, as this helps to set the tone and pace for the event. Some trainers use music to help to create a positive atmosphere at the start of the programme.
- Get people involved. Use an ice-breaker (see Chapter 3) to help people settle down and relax into the session. The sooner individuals are engaged with a small group of colleagues, the quicker they will relax and participate in whole-group activities.
- Grab people's interest. Use stories, appropriate humour, a video clip or quick quiz to grab people's attention and interest in the session.

Training events can start off badly if the trainer does the following:

- Fails to prepare the room, facilities or equipment. Starting a session by focusing on sorting out technical issues or asking delegates to move furniture is not conducive to creating a positive and professional learning environment.
- Looks unprofessional. If the trainer is scruffily dressed or looks unprofessional, then the participants may make assumptions about his/her professionalism and ability to run the session. If in doubt, dress formally rather than informally.
- Starts with negative comments. If trainers start off with negative comments, this will create a negative atmosphere and make it hard for some people to fully engage with the training event. Examples of unacceptable comments include:
  — I've been asked to do this at the last minute and I haven't had time to prepare.
  — I hope you won't find this as boring as the last group.
  — I don't know about you, but I would prefer to be watching the Olympics rather than running this course.
  — I always hate training in this room it is too small and overheats.

- Starts late. Starting late means getting off to a bad start and may make it difficult to manage timing for the whole event. Sometimes it is impossible to start on time, e.g. half the group may be late due to problems with public transport. In this case, it is worthwhile explaining the situation to the group and saying when you will start: 'Thank you for being here on time. It is now time to start but half the group is late. We will give them an additional 10 minutes and then we will begin.'
- Starts too slowly. If you get off to a slow start, e.g. your introductions lack energy, or administrative activities take longer than required, then it can be difficult to re-energize the group. Sometimes introducing an additional game or a stand-up activity (see Chapter 3) will help you to retain control over the pace of the event.

Different ways of involving everyone in the training process

The following list identifies different ways of involving everyone in the training process.

- Ask everyone to introduce themselves and say what they want to gain from the course. Write this up on a flipchart or whiteboard. At the end of the session, refer back to this information and check that everyone has achieved their aims.
- Use an introductory activity or ice-breaker.
- Use people's names throughout the session.
- Refer to comments that participants have made earlier in the training session.
- Show your interest and enthusiasm through your verbal and body language.
- Treat everyone with respect.
- Be culturally sensitive.
- If anyone has additional needs, then check that you have made appropriate adjustments for them.
- Ask people to work in different groups, e.g. pairs, trios and quads.
- Have breaks and give people the opportunity to go outside for a few minutes.
- Use real-life stories.
- Use different activities which engage different senses, e.g. sight, sound and touch.
- Use games.
- Use rewards, e.g. sweets, fresh fruit, small items of stationery.
- Ensure that everyone feels noticed and cared about.
- Give lots of praise and encouragement.

Managing the learning process

As a trainer, it is important for you to manage the learning process and to balance the needs of individuals and the whole group so that you achieve your training goals and learning outcomes. This normally involves:

- following the session plan
- monitoring the participants – individuals, small groups, whole groups – and noting their energy levels, enthusiasm and anyone who appears disinterested or dissatisfied
- monitoring the room – temperature, fresh air, any intrusive noise
- managing and controlling the group.

Table 6.1 provides guidance on interventions in response to different situations which can occur during the training session.

Table 6.1 *Training interventions*	
Training situation	**Potential interventions**
Low-energy group	• Change the pace. Speed it up. Use an interested and excited tone of voice. Move about more • Ask the participants to do an exercise that involves getting out of their seats • Use activities that involve competition, excitement and humour • Use loud music • Have a break. Encourage people to go outside • Creative handshakes. Ask everyone to shake hands with at least two other people, each time inventing a new form of handshake • Set up a quiz. Ask each team to work out 20 questions and then run the quiz
High-energy group	• Slow down your pace and breathing • Introduce an individual activity, e.g. reading a brief article, completing a quiz • Give the group a very challenging activity • Tell the group a story • Make a slow explanation of a key topic
Individuals focused on an external issue	• Use the same strategies as for the low-energy group • Ask the individuals about the external issue and then ask them to leave it on one side until the end of the training event • Suggest that they leave the training event
Major disruption, e.g. fire alarm, serious illness	• Assess whether or not there is sufficient time to resume the training session • If it is impossible to resume the session, then send everyone an e-mail with all learning resources and advice on what to do next • If the training event is resumed then give everyone a few minutes to settle down and ask them to forget about the interruption and focus on the rest of the training event. You will need to work through the programme more quickly in order to catch up on lost time

Questions

Questions are an important part of any training event and they may be asked by the trainer or the delegates. Trainers may use questions as a means of:

- facilitating the learning process
- assessing learning
- obtaining information and ideas
- clarifying a problem or issue
- finding out someone's requirements.

Used appropriately, questions can really facilitate the learning process and help to produce an engaging and challenging training event. Some common dos and don'ts for asking questions are given in Table 6.2.

Table 6.2 *Dos and don'ts for asking questions*

Do	Don't
Ask questions	Make statements that sound like questions – it causes confusion
Ask one question at a time	Ask multiple questions
Make it clear whether the question is aimed at one person or the whole group	Ask rhetorical questions
Ask short questions	Ask leading questions
Be open to the answer you receive	Ask long and rambling questions
Remain neutral to the answer	Be judgemental of the response or use phrases such as 'that's right' or 'that's wrong'
Use all your listening skills to make sure that you understand the response	Expect participants to read your mind and know the answer you are expecting
If necessary, repeat the answer to make sure that you have understood it	

As the trainer, it is up to you to manage questions from your delegates. In general, new trainers often find it easiest to leave question time until the end of the session, as this helps them to manage the time. More experienced trainers welcome questions throughout the training session. Strategies for managing questions include:

- Let delegates know your approach to managing questions – do you welcome them at any time in the training event, or will you allocate a particular time for questions?
- When someone asks a question, make sure that you understand it. Repeat the question as a means of checking your understanding, and also to make sure that everyone has heard it.
- Answer the question. If you don't know the answer, then say so and tell the delegates how you will find out the answer.

- If time is short, then indicate how many questions you will deal with: 'We have time for two more questions.'
- If one person is dominating the question time, then give others an opportunity to ask questions: 'Thank you for all your questions, but I want to give other delegates a chance to ask their questions.'
- If no one asks any questions, then use strategies to generate questions, as illustrated in the following examples:
  — In a small training group, e.g. 10 to 16 delegates, pass out sticky notes and ask participants to work in pairs or trios. Their task is to identify at least one question, write it on the sticky note and hand it to the trainer. The trainer then deals with the questions.
  — In a large group, e.g. 50 to 500 students in an information skills session, ask everyone to work with their neighbour and identify a question. Ask them to write the question on a piece of paper and pass it to the front. The trainer then deals with the questions. If there is insufficient time to answer them all, the questions and their answers can be posted on the VLE.
  — In a large group, e.g. 50 to 500 students in an information skills session, ask everyone to text in their question(s) to a mobile phone number used by the trainer. The trainer then deals with the questions. If there is insufficient time to answer them all, the questions and their answers can be posted on the VLE.

The topic of managing questions in the context of lectures or presentations is also covered in Chapter 3.

Ending the learning process

It is important to provide an 'ending' to the learning process, as this helps people attending the training session to complete that stage and move on to their next activity. Typically, the final stages of a training event may involve the following activities:

- summary of main learning points
- action planning (see Chapter 3)
- course evaluation (see Chapter 5)
- formal ending of the course.

Different ways of summarizing the main learning points include:

- the trainer providing a summary
- individuals or small groups producing a mind map or spider diagram (see Chapter 4) of their main learning points

- individuals or small groups providing a summary of one aspect of the course for the whole group
- small groups developing a quiz based on the course content and then 'testing' their peers
- the trainer running a quiz with different teams competing against each other.

It is important to end the training session formally by:

- clearly stating that it has come to an end
- providing contact details
- thanking delegates.

Teaching large groups

Different trainers have different perspectives on what is a large group, but it tends to range from 30 to 800 people. This is often in the context of college or university education. If you are asked to work with a large group, there are some key questions to ask:

- Is there a choice of room?
- How do you engage with a large audience?
- How do individuals participate?
- How do you control the group and manage tricky situations?
- How do you respond to the needs of a diverse group of people?
- How do you get your message across?

With very large groups, there is often no choice of room, and this means that you must make the best of the room allocated. As mentioned earlier in this chapter, it is important to check out the learning environment and, as much as possible, to manage it so that it suits your needs. In some situations, e.g. running a training event in a large hall or theatre in a school or college, it is helpful to work with a colleague, as this means that one person can concentrate on managing the group while the other deals with the technology.

Mass lectures

Many library and information workers deliver mass lectures to large groups of people. Typically a mass lecture will be delivered using one or more tools such as PowerPoint, live ICT demonstrations, interactive whiteboard or video clips (see Chapter 4). During a lecture (and other learning activities) concentration and retention of information is not constant. Typically it drops off over time and this means that introducing activities helps to improve concentration and recall of information. Consequently, it is a good idea to include one or more activities during a lecture to help to improve motivation and student participation. Common advice given to new lecturers is to provide some kind of change, e.g. an activity, after 20 minutes, as typically the students' concentration will start to fade then.

Activities need to be carefully managed, otherwise they can either take up too much time or fizzle out like a damp squib. Managing activities involves providing very clear instructions, given both verbally and visually using PowerPoint, and then making it clear when you want the students to start and end their activity. In mass lectures you need to use very clear commands such as 'start the activity **NOW**' and 'please **END** the activity **NOW**'. I find it helpful to flash or lower the lights in the lecture room, e.g. to give a few seconds' warning of the beginning of an activity, and then flash or lower the lights again at the end of the activity. This use of non-verbal stimuli helps to make it very clear that you are moving on to the next part of the activity or lecture.

A wide range of activities (outlined in Chapter 3) can be used within a lecture. Examples outlined below include:

- quizzes
- case studies or other activities
- interviews
- mini-discussions
- question-and-answer sessions
- action planning.

Quizzes (see Chapters 3 and 4) can be used in a variety of ways within a lecture, as shown by the following examples:

- A paper-based diagnostic quiz can be placed on each chair, and the students can be asked to complete it as they arrive. As the tutor, you can then ask for answers using a show of hands. This is a useful starting activity because it can be used to identify the levels of knowledge within the group and so to inform the rest of the lecture. However, this type of activity does need careful handling so that it doesn't become too long and drawn out.
- Quizzes involving simple multiple-choice or true and false questions can be included in the presentation. Answers can be generated in a number of ways: by show of hands; by use of different coloured cards; or using an audience response system.
- A paper-based quiz can be used part way through the lecture, and then the audience are asked to mark each other's answers as the tutor works through the correct answers.

If you use this type of activity, then remember to include sufficient time for people with special needs to complete it. The lecture can be followed up with an online quiz in a VLE or an e-mail quiz, and a prize can be offered for the first five correct sets of answers that are chosen at random.

Case study 6.1 Evaluating information sources

An information skills trainer working in a university used the following activity, presented as part of a PowerPoint presentation, in her introductory information skills lectures. First she would ask the students to work in pairs or threes on the following task:

List the following in terms of academic credibility:

1 Newspaper article (*The Times*)
2 Textbook
3 Journal article (refereed)
4 Journal article (not refereed)
5 Conference paper (American Academy of Management)
6 Government report.

Then she would ask them to raise their hands to indicate which of the six items they had ranked top in terms of academic credibility. This always caused some discussion. She then presented her own list as follows:

1 Journal article (refereed)
2 Conference paper (American Academy of Management)
3 Newspaper article (*The Times*)
4 Journal article (not refereed)
5 Textbook
6 Government report.

This activity normally worked well and provided a good source for discussion with the students.

TIP FOR TRAINERS

Case studies and other activities can be used to enliven a mass lecture. Examples include:

- a mini-case study given as part of a PowerPoint presentation
- asking the audience members to rank information sources in terms of quality and/or relevance
- anagrams or word puzzles
- quizzes.

See Chapter 3 for additional activities.

Guests

Interviewing guests can provide a welcome change within a lecture. My own experience is that many people don't like speaking in front of very large groups, and to facilitate this process I often suggest that I interview them as part of the lecture, or I ask a couple of students to interview them. This works well, as it offers a different type of activity within the lecture and the guest speaker often feels more comfortable being interviewed rather than speaking to the whole group. I ask students who did the course the previous year to come along and be interviewed. This is often very valuable, as they put over important messages about academic skills in a way that has great credibility. Finally, whenever possible I record these interviews using a digital recorder and then upload the file to the VLE or e-mail it to students.

Mini-discussions

Mini-discussions (see more about discussions in Chapter 3) can be used within lectures, e.g. asking students to discuss specific ideas in twos or threes and then sharing their findings and thoughts with another group. One way of facilitating this process is to provide every student with a sticky note (it can be stuck under their seat before they arrive) and ask them to write down one thought that they have on the subject and then to swap sticky notes three times so that each person has a note whose writer cannot be identified. Then ask specific students to read out the thoughts on the note and use this to generate discussion.

Question-and-answer sessions

Question-and-answer sessions are traditionally held at the end of a lecture, although it is often useful to include opportunities for questions at the end of each theme. If you introduce a question-and-answer session, then remember that you control the question time. It is useful at the start of a lecture to say when and how you will handle questions. If you do ask for questions, give the students time to think of and ask them. I often silently count to ten so as to give people thinking time. There are a number of techniques that can be used to generate questions. One popular technique is to ask students to talk with their neighbours and to give them three or four minutes to identify any outstanding questions or points that require clarification. You can then ask them to write their questions on pre-circulated sticky notes or cards. Collect in the questions and answer them. If there are any questions that you can't answer, then say that you will post the question and answer online.

Action planning

Action planning is a useful activity at the end of a lecture, when the trainer asks everyone to identify and write down one thing that they will do differently as a result of the lecture. Ask them to set a SMART outcome (see Chapter 3). You may want to provide them with a sticky note or a structure for their action plan via a PowerPoint presentation. Typical examples could include actions such as: use advanced search facilities when next searching academic databases; explore the use of citation-indexing tools; read the relevant chapter in an appropriate textbook. Once the students have written down their action point, then ask them to share it with a neighbour. This type of activity takes only a few minutes but helps the students to put into practice their learning from the session.

Case study 6.2 Giving out handouts

Circulating handouts in a mass lecture can be very time consuming and one mistake I made a number of years ago was to attempt to hand out a paper-based quiz to 500 students half way through a lecture. It took almost 10 minutes and I had lost the audience's attention by the time everyone had received their handout. This meant that I then had to work harder to refocus the students. What I learnt from the experience was that it is worthwhile handing out materials before the start of a lecture, and I often ask a colleague to help me to do this, as it speeds up the whole process. I also find that colour-coding materials is helpful, as during the lecture you can refer to specific handouts by their colour and this helps to smooth the whole process of students moving into an activity.

Case study 6.3 Using the Cephalonian method

Jane, an information skills librarian, uses the Cephalonian method with her first-year undergraduate students. It involves planting questions in the audience. Jane prepares a set of cards, each containing one question. She then hands them out to selected students as they come into the lecture theatre. During the lecture, at set times, she asks the individuals to read out the questions, which she then answers. Jane says that it helps students' engagement and encourages them to ask questions. Jane obtained the idea from reading Morgan and Davies (2004).

Case study 6.4 Teaching information skills

Sandra, a liaison librarian, is responsible for information skills teaching in a business school. Each year she teaches 500 first-year undergraduate students topics such as business information sources, evaluating information sources and referencing.

As part of induction, Sandra lectures for 30 minutes to the first-year students and introduces them to the library, basic business information sources and the importance of the e-book collection. This session is introduced by the director of undergraduate studies, who stays in the room the whole time. Sandra uses a PowerPoint presentation which includes two video clips: the first is of a second-year student talking about using the library and academic sources in order to gain high grades; the second is of an international student talking about the importance of using the library, and the help that library staff can provide to students.

Sandra maintains tight control of the students – if anyone talks, then she stops speaking and waits for silence before continuing. She maintains a good pace and is formal but friendly with the students. At the end of the session, she says that she is looking forward to working with the students during the year and helping them to be successful in their degrees.

Following on from induction, Sandra gives 10-minute presentations as part of a core module, 'Academic and Professional Skills', and she uses these to inform the students of key information sources and ideas. The presentations are backed up by a site in the VLE which provides background information, examples and case studies, and more video clips where students talk about their experiences.

Asked what tips she would give to other trainers dealing with large groups of students, Sandra said: 'Wherever possible, have an academic in the room with you and ask them to introduce you. This helps the students to make the link between information skills and their course. It also helps with managing behaviour.'

Making database training interesting

Database training can be quite difficult to deliver, as the subject is technical and there is sometimes a tendency to spend too much time on presentations which deliver too much detail. As with any other training event, database training can be enlivened by using a number of different learning and teaching techniques, including:

- short presentations by the trainer
- individuals or pairs making presentations
- hands-on activities
- activities for individuals, pairs or trios
- games, quizzes or tests.

Chapter 3 outlines a wide range of learning and teaching methods, e.g. teaching Boolean logic through an exercise based on what people had for their breakfast (see under Activities), or using games. Specific examples of using technologies to support training are provided in Chapter 4. Some additional examples relevant to database training include:

- using video clips of 'experts' commenting on the database
- using obscure and entertaining examples of articles or other resources (but be careful not to offend anyone)
- setting up a game, e.g. ask individuals or pairs to complete a question sheet – the first person/pair to complete it receives a small prize
- bringing in a guest and interviewing them
- developing a board game
- using an online quiz
- giving people a five-minute break and asking them to go outside in pairs and come back with one question relating to the database.

Case study 6.5 Timeline for an engaging database training session

Figure 6.1 provides an overview of the activities involved in an engaging database training session delivered by one of the major database suppliers. This was a one-hour session and the trainer includes seven different training activities. Some of them were predictable: 1, 4, 5 and 7, while others are less commonly used in database training sessions: quiz, video clip and pub quiz. However, the whole event worked, and this was largely due to the trainer's skills and his ability to develop and maintain an energetic and well-paced training session.

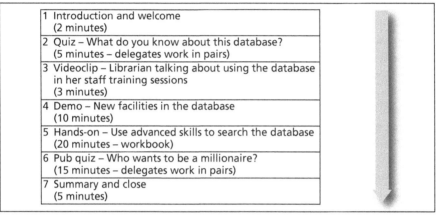

Figure 6.1 *Timeline for an engaging database training session*

Case study 6.6 Engaging database training sessions

Carbery and Hegarty (2010), based at the Waterford Institute of Technology (WIT) in Ireland, describe an approach to delivering engaging database training sessions to first-year students. This involved developing worksheets, as outlined in the following extract:

In an effort to introduce stimulating elements of activity and fun into the training, we developed a number of learning materials, or worksheets, for teaching database-searching skills. All of the paper-based worksheets are designed to be user-friendly and visually appealing. Designed and produced in-house, they contain text, graphics and screen captures, as well as 'Top tip' boxes emphasizing important features and techniques. Once completed, we invite students to keep their worksheets so that they can refer back when applying the search techniques in their own database usage.

These learning materials are created for core database resources that the library subscribes to, such as Science Direct, Emerald, ABI/Inform and Wiley Online Library, amongst others. The worksheets are based on the main subject areas taught within WIT, in an effort to tailor and customize them to the students themselves.

As a method of captivating students' interest, we decided to create learning materials that emulate popular television programmes. 'The Apprentice', 'CSI' and 'Dragons' Den' have all helped us teach students how to search for scholarly research articles on the library databases. In the case of business and management students, they find themselves completing a worksheet that sees them depicted as contestants on 'The Apprentice', and in order to secure the job, they need to hone their research skills. With the 'CSI' worksheet … the science student is a forensic scientist trying to solve a tough crime case. If students succeed in completing the worksheet, they solve the case! Drawing on TV shows allows us to create fun, innovative worksheets, with a narrative throughout. Although they are often set in whimsical and fantastic scenarios, the worksheet themes can help showcase the use of research skills and scholarly research outside of a purely academic, essay-led environment. Our brief when designing any database worksheet is to make it fun, engaging and inventive.

Regardless of the TV show or database chosen, all of the worksheets follow a consistent pattern, covering the following sections:

- basic keyword search
- advanced keyword search (including Boolean searching and other search options)
- browsing for publications.

Adopting elements of active, student-centred learning through specially designed, interactive learning materials has been a success for us in WIT libraries. By designing worksheets based on popular television programmes, we aim to teach database searching and other research skills in a fun, memorable way.

Example 6.1 Outline database training session
Table 6.3 shows how one trainer organized a database training session which involved a one-hour face-to-face session. This was a lunchtime session aimed at staff working within the health service.

Table 6.3 Outline database training session	
Before the start of the training session	Send delegates a welcome e-mail. Ask them to complete a short quiz (six questions) about their experience of using the database, and also their subject(s) of interest
During the training session	5 minutes – welcome, introductions and housekeeping arrangements 5 minutes – presentation outlining the key features of the database 20 minutes – hands-on session using a series of activities on a handout 10 minutes – pair activity: completing a quiz about the features of the database 5 minutes – debriefing quiz 5 minutes – question-and-answer session 5 minutes – summary, plus mention of other features (which will be covered in the next lunchtime course) 5 minutes – close of session, show access to website with additional materials, provide contact details and information about drop-in sessions
After the training session	Send an e-mail with a link to an evaluation questionnaire (four questions) and also a link to the website with additional resources

Working with challenging learners

Every trainer is likely to experience occasional participants whom s/he experiences as difficult, and this may be the result of the participant(s):

- not wanting to attend the course
- having low expectations about the course
- feeling uncomfortable with the tutor
- feeling uncomfortable with one or more participants
- feeling uncomfortable with environment (either face-to-face and/or online)
- being distracted by factors in the workplace (e.g. forthcoming disciplinary meeting, forthcoming merger, restructuring of department)
- being distracted by factors outside the workplace (e.g. argument with partner, family health problems, debt problems).

Many of these factors have nothing to do with the trainer, but, if s/he does not manage the situation, they can adversely affect the whole learning process and training event. Common difficulties affecting the whole group may include:

- one or more participants taking over learning activities
- one or more participants not joining in
- participants having private conversations
- individuals being excluded by the group
- disagreement leading to confrontation
- one or more individuals attempting to sabotage the activity or programme.

In some groups, one or more participants may dominate discussions and question time, and this may result in others not contributing. Possible ways of handling such situations include:

- setting up appropriate ground rules at the start of the programme, session or activity
- acknowledging their contribution and asking for someone else to contribute
- acknowledging their contribution and pointing out that everyone needs an opportunity to speak
- structuring discussions and feedback sessions so that everyone has an equal opportunity to speak
- giving them a task, e.g. observe and report back, so that they focus on this during a discussion
- letting the group handle it.

Sometimes one or more people will not participate in the course, e.g. as a result of more senior staff being present, because they feel that they have nothing to contribute, or because they need more time to think. Possible ways of handling this situation include:

- giving them more time
- setting up small-group work and ensuring that everyone has an opportunity to report back
- making eye contact and asking for their views.

Another problem is when individuals start talking amongst themselves. There are two main types of side conversations: those which are about the course content and which take place through the participants' interest and enthusiasm; and those which have nothing to do with the course and are, perhaps, a sign of boredom. Possible ways to handle this include:

- setting appropriate ground rules at the start of the session
- stopping people talking and waiting for them to be quiet before proceeding
- asking them to share their conversation with the whole group
- asking them a direct question.

The final common type of difficult situation is when there is a major disagreement occurs between one or more participants and the rest of the group. This can be handled in a number of ways:

- Take control immediately.
- Never take sides.
- Interrupt the discussion with a direct question and refocus them on the training materials.
- Bring another participant into the discussion.
- Summarize the differences and state that everyone is entitled to their own opinion, and then move on to a new topic.
- Ask everyone to summarize their position, using evidence to support it, and then ask them to 'agree to disagree' (this has the added value of their actually agreeing about something!).
- Change the subject.
- Speak to the people concerned in private, e.g. outside of the training room, or by phone if it relates to an online element of the programme.

Many trainers work with large groups in educational institutions, schools, colleges or universities, and so they have to develop skills for working with difficult behaviours. Table 6.4 outlines some of these strategies.

Table 6.4 *Dealing with difficult behaviours in large groups*

Situation	Strategy
Chattering students	• The trainer should stop talking and make eye contact with the students. Ask them if they have any queries relating to the training session. If not, then ask them to respect their colleagues – chattering is distracting for both students and trainers. If the situation continues, then ask the students to leave your session and report their behaviour to their tutor.
Large numbers of late students	• Leave the first few rows empty and ask the students to sit there. Don't repeat the first part of the session for them. Explain how they can catch up at the end of the session. • Either ask a colleague to stay outside the room or put up a poster on the door(s) saying that late-comers are not admitted. • Ask your institution to introduce and monitor a policy that does not permit late entry to learning and teaching sessions. This type of policy is becoming increasingly common.
Someone tries to take over your session, e.g. by constantly asking questions	• Explain that their questions are disrupting your flow and suggest they ask them at the end or come along to a drop-in session.
Mobile phones keep going off	• Ask everyone to turn off their mobiles or turn them to silent mode.
Students use laptops and/or mobile phones throughout the session	• Ignore them. They may be using their devices as learning tools.
People walk out	• Ignore them. Afterwards you may want to find out if there was something related to your session that made them walk out. They may have left due to transport or child- or adult-care issues.
Strong disagreement	• If there is strong disagreement about the content of your session then it may be sensible 'to agree to disagree' or to say that you will continue the discussion after the end of the session.

Example 6.2 Managing late-comers

How do you deal with late-comers? This is a common question which arises in discussions about running training sessions. Basically, the trainer needs to decide how to manage this situation. The following examples indicate some different approaches to dealing with this situation.

• Mark is a trainer who works in a library service which covers one of the largest counties in the UK. He holds training sessions in four different venues, but some people may have an hour's journey to attend the event. There are normally one or two late-comers. Mark always starts his sessions on time. As late-comers arrive, he welcomes them and says that he will catch up with them in the break.

- Alison runs induction sessions for groups of 30 to 50 students in a further education college. She makes sure that the front rows in the lecture theatre are kept empty and she directs late-comers to these seats. This means that they don't disrupt other people by trying to move to empty seats in the middle of rows. Alison doesn't make any allowances for late arrivals, but makes sure that all learning resources and guides are available on the college's VLE.
- Bushra works for a database provider and often runs training sessions for librarians and information workers about the resources. She provides late-comers with a copy of her PowerPoint presentation and says that she will discuss the missed elements with them during the break.

When dealing with late-comers, it is normally not a good idea to repeat the element of the course that has been missed. This is boring and repetitive for people who arrived on time. If there is a trickle of late-comers, then the repetition can really disrupt the session, irritate the people who were on time, and mess up the timing.

Summary

Delivering face-to-face training events can be summed up in a few sentences:

1 Know where you are going (the aim and learning outcomes)
2 Know how to get there (the session plan)
3 Know how to deliver the training session. This involves managing the group and its learning processes, including:
   a. Getting started
   b. Delivering the training session
   c. Ending the training session.

Points 1 and 2 were covered in Chapter 5. This chapter has focused on delivering the training session and managing the overall learning processes. It has covered the topics of getting started, managing the learning process, questions and ending the learning process. The chapter has also covered the topics of teaching large groups, making database training interesting and working with challenging learners. An important point is to be flexible and to respond to your delegates.

References and additional resources

Buckley, R. and Caple, J. (2009) *The Theory and Practice of Training*, Kogan Page.
Cameron, E. (2005) *Facilitation Made Easy*, Kogan Page.
Carbery, A. and Hegarty, N. (2010) Think 'on' the Box: delivering engaging library database training to first year undergraduate students, *SCONUL Newsletter*, **50**, 52–5, www.sconul.ac.uk/publications/newsletter/50/15.rtf [accessed on 28 August 2012].
Langan, K. (2011) Training Millennials: a practical and theoretical approach, *Reference*

Services Review, **40** (1), 24–48.

Morgan, N. and Davies, L. (2004) Innovative Library Induction – introducing the 'Cephalonian Method', *SCONUL Newsletter*, www.sconul.ac.uk/publications/newsletter/32/2.rtf [accessed on 12 August 2012].

7

E-learning and blended learning

Introduction

The purpose of this chapter is to bring together different ideas and approaches to e-learning and blended learning. Figure 7.1 provides a simple overview of the relationships between face-to-face, blended learning and e-learning. Individual training programmes will be positioned somewhere along this continuum.

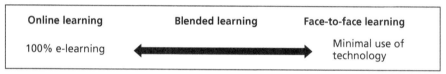

Figure 7.1 *Overview of blended learning*

The chapter starts with a focus on e-learning and discusses the design of two different types of e-learning programmes: web-based tutorials and learning groups and communities. This is then followed by sections on blended learning and the design of blended learning programmes. Working in an online environment requires a different skill-set to delivering face-to-face sessions, and this is explored in the section on e-tutoring. The chapter concludes with a section on evaluating e-learning and blended learning.

E-learning

E-learning refers to learning or development that is delivered or mediated through the use of online technologies. Increasingly, many organizations are using 100% e-learning, i.e. web-based training programmes, as a means of ensuring that staff have completed mandatory training on subjects such as health and safety, diversity training. However, blended learning, which involves face-to-face interactions either in the same place or over the internet (described in the next section) does appear to be becoming more popular than 100% e-learning.

The advantages of e-learning for different people are often quoted as follows:

- for the learner:
  — doesn't involve travel or time away from the workplace/home
  — learns at own pace
  — easy to fit into schedule.
- for the manager:
  — saves on travel costs and individuals being away from workplace
  — easy to fit into workplace schedules
  — easy to demonstrate that people have completed e-learning course and have achieved required learning outcomes, e.g. through online testing.

The disadvantages of e-learning include:

- the cost of producing high quality e-learning programmes
- some people are not enthusiastic about this approach to training
- unless individuals are provided with 'protected time', they may find that they don't have time to complete the e-learning programme, or their pressure at work increases
- it can be difficult to ensure that individuals complete the programmes.

Chapter 4 provides an extensive range of examples of the ways in which e-learning can be used to deliver training. They can be divided into trainer- or content-centred approaches and student-centred or social approaches to learning (see Chapter 2). Content-centred approaches to training using traditional web-based tools include:

- use of aggregators, e.g. Google Reader, Netvibes, Pageflakes
- blogging, e.g. use of Blogger, Livejournal, Typepad, WordPress
- web-based training
- use of videos and other multimedia such as live streaming, e.g. justin.tv or Livestream
- quizzes and surveys.

Student-centred approaches and social approaches to learning tend to overlap and frequently involve the use of Web 2.0 tools. Examples include:

- social networking, e.g. use of LinkedIn
- conferencing, e.g. GoToMeet, Skype
- collaboration tools:
  — meetings, e.g. use of Adobe ConnectNow, Groupboard, Google Groups, ShowMyPC
  — project management tools, e.g. Joyent, Project2Manage, Taskada
  — social bibliography, e.g. CiteULike, Mendeley

— social bookmarking, e.g. Delicious, Diigo
— social documents, e.g. Google Docs, Dropbox
— wikis, e.g. PBworks, Wetpaint, Wikia
— virtual worlds, e.g. Second Life.

These online tools and technologies are described in more detail in Chapter 4.

Case study 7.1 Learning how to use an in-house IT system

Jonathan was appointed as an administrator in a workplace library in a City of London finance company. Part of his duties included managing the information centre's finances, and for this he needed to use an internal system called FinFast. He sent an e-mail to the finance manager asking for help in learning how to use the system. In reply he received an e-mail giving him a basic online tutorial to follow. Once he had completed the tutorial he received another e-mail with more advanced guidance. This was sufficient for him to get started with FinFast. Over the next few weeks he sent a few e-mails to the finance manager asking for help, and this enabled him to learn the required functions of the system.

Design of e-learning programmes

The design of e-learning training starts off in exactly the same way as for face-to-face events, i.e. by working out the training aim and learning outcomes (see Chapter 5). It is then necessary to work out the learning and training process, and this will vary depending on whether the training medium is a web-based tutorial or a learning group or community.

Web-based tutorials

The development of a web-based training tutorial will involve producing a similar structure to that used in face-to-face sessions (see Chapter 5):

1 Basic introduction
2 Indication of the benefits of completing the tutorial, using techniques such as:
   a. video clip recommendations from previous users
   b. text-based recommendations from previous users
   c. diagnostic test.
3 Description of the topic, using techniques such as:
   a. text
   b. multimedia clips
   c. additional materials, e.g. audio or video files, MS Word or PDF files.
4 Activities – these may be online or learners may be asked to complete an activity in their library or using an online database. Example activities include:
   a. self-assessment tests
   b. worksheets or other activities to be completed
   c. suggestions of further work.

5 Question time:
  a. frequently asked questions
  b. opportunity to send e-mails to a trainer.
6 Summary, e.g. video clip, diagrams, etc.
7 Close of tutorial. Thank you and production of any certificates or results of tests.

This structure follows the 4MAT approach (see Chapter 5, Table 5.3). In terms of designing web-based tutorials, it is important to ensure that they have the following characteristics:

- are visually attractive
- have clear and accessibly written text
- have clear navigation routes with options for moving forwards, backwards and jumping sections
- use visual, auditory and kinaesthetic learning resources and activities (the VAK learning styles model)
- provide opportunities for interaction and feedback
- are accessible to people with special needs (see Chapter 5)
- are accessible on a wide range of technologies, e.g. smartphones, laptops, tablets, etc.

TIP FOR TRAINERS

Producing and developing a web-based tutorial is an expensive and time-consuming project. You need to make sure that you have a range of resources and skills available to you, including technical support, web-authoring skills, multimedia skills, knowledge of learning and teaching, knowledge of the subject content of the tutorial. If you do not have access to these resources and skills, then you may end up producing a poor-quality tutorial. There are so many excellent tutorials already available that perhaps you could use one of them. Remember to obtain permission from the copyright owner. ■

Case study 7.2 Online induction in a university library

Elston and Schneider (2011, 31) describe the development of an online induction programme in a university library. This was an interesting project, as a graduate trainee played a central role in it and led focus groups with different groups of library staff. This resulted in agreement that:

> the content would be mostly generic but would highlight the subject-specific support available to students through 'talking head' videos which would provide individual introductions to each librarian as well as pointing students to their library subject support pages. In addition there was a consensus that the induction should use a range of technologies and approaches, particularly screen-capture software and videos to engage the students and ensure that dense text was kept to a minimum.

The tool Articulate Studio, which integrates with other software such as Captivate, was used to develop the online induction.

The evaluations received were very positive:

> *The response to the induction was very positive, with 100% of respondents saying they would recommend it to a friend. Students generally found the navigation simple to use as highlighted by comments including 'I love the layout; it is easy to find the resources I want', 'it is quite clear and well structured by dividing into different subjects'. Students also found the screen captures and demonstration videos particularly helpful and requested more. The amount of interactivity as well as the level of information provided was felt to be about right for an induction resource. The focus groups agreed, however, that more subject specific advice would improve the induction, such as a video tour showing where the books on their subject were housed in the library.*
>
> (Elston and Schneider, 2011, 33)

The Skills@Library induction package is available from http://skills.library.leeds.ac.uk/induction.

Learning groups and communities

As outlined in Chapter 2, learning is a social process, and it is possible to design online training events which are based on groups of people working together. At the heart of these programmes is the idea that a group of people come together in a virtual environment to develop their knowledge and skills. This has the advantage of enabling library and information workers to come together in a virtual team and learn from each other. Typically, this type of course may involve participants coming together in a virtual space from different regions, countries or continents. The programme may be focused on a particular sector, e.g. schools, law or health services, or be open to any librarian or information worker.

Gilly Salmon (2000) provides a helpful outline of the development of an online group. Her model is adapted here to represent what commonly happens in library and information online learning groups or communities. The model involves a number of stages which form the structure of the online learning event:

1 Access and motivation
2 Online socialization
3 Information exchange
4 Group learning activity or project work
5 Informing
6 Closure.

This model provides a design structure for an online group programme which will guide participants through a series of activities which reflect Stages 1 to 6. In order to encourage an effective online learning group or community, here are some examples of the types of activities in which a trainer is likely to be involved:

Stage 1: Access and motivation

- Ensure that the online group is set up with a welcome message.
- Ensure that group members know how to access the online group.
- Open a discussion group.

Stage 2: Online socialization

- Lead a round of introductions with, perhaps, an online ice-breaker.
- Welcome new group members or late arrivals.
- Provide a structure for getting started, e.g. agreement of group rules.
- If individuals break the agreed group netiquette, then address the issue (either privately or through the discussion group).
- Wherever possible avoid playing 'ping pong' with individual group members and ask other people for their opinions and ideas.
- Encourage quieter group members to join in.
- Provide summaries of online discussions. This is called weaving and involves summarizing and synthesizing the content of multiple responses in a virtual group.

Stage 3: Information exchange

- Provide highly structured activities at the start of the group's life.
- Encourage participation.
- Ask questions.
- Encourage group members to post short messages.
- Allocate online roles to individual members, e.g. to provide a summary of a particular thread of discussion.
- Close off threads as and when appropriate.
- Encourage the online group to develop its own life and history. Welcome shared language, metaphors, rituals and jokes.

Stage 4: Group learning activity or project work

- Facilitate online activities.
- Monitor process with respect to the project plan.
- Facilitate the process.
- Ask questions.

- Encourage reflection.

Stage 5: Informing

- Facilitate an online (or face-to-face) dissemination activity.
- Give feedback.
- Ask questions.
- Encourage reflection.

Stage 6: Closure

- Ensure that 'loose ends' are completed.
- Highlight group achievements.
- Encourage (structured) reflection on and evaluation of group process.
- Thank group members for their contributions and work.
- Formally close the activity (or programme).

Table 7.1 provides a summary of tutor and participant activities in an online group learning programme.

Table 7.1 *Model of group or community learning and development process (adapted from Salmon, 2000)*		
Stage	**Tutor activities**	**Group member activities**
1 Access and motivation	• Welcome and encouragement • Guidance on where to find technical support	• Accessing the system • Finding their way around
2 Online socialization	• Introductions • Ice-breakers • Ground rules • Netiquette	• Sending and receiving messages • Getting to know each other • Starting to develop a group culture
3 Information exchange	• Facilitating structured activities • Assigning roles and responsibilities • Encouraging discussions • Summarizing findings and/or outcomes	• Exploring roles, responsibilities, project tasks • Carrying out activities • Reporting and discussing findings
4 Project or learning activities	• Facilitating online activities • Monitoring process with respect to overall programme • Facilitating the process • Asking questions • Encouraging reflection	• Completing project tasks or learning activities • Giving and receiving feedback • Problem solving
5 Informing	• Facilitating the process • Asking questions • Encouraging reflection	• Disseminating findings • Giving and receiving feedback • Reflecting on outcomes and learning process
6 Closure	• Leading review and evaluation process • Ensuring that loose ends are completed • Leading closure	• Completing all tasks and activities • Completing review and evaluation processes • Goodbyes

Blended learning

Blended learning involves a combination of face-to-face and e-learning activities and frequently involves using different internet-based tools, including chat rooms, discussion groups, podcasts and self-assessment tools, to support a traditional course. Increasingly, blended learning is becoming a normal method of training, as individuals are using a combination of face-to-face training and online methods even if the latter involve simply providing e-mail support or access to additional learning resources.

Reasons for developing and delivering blended learning training programmes include:

- making learning more accessible, engaging and relevant
- providing more flexible learning opportunities
- reducing the amount of time spent on face-to-face learning activities
- integrating practitioner-based experiences with classroom-based learning
- developing programmes that are relatively cheap to repeat or use with large groups of learners
- exploiting ICT and training facilities
- demonstrating the use of leading-edge technologies
- demand from users or other stakeholders
- interest at senior management level
- availability of external funding
- to explore new approaches to learning and teaching.

Blended learning programmes may include:

- a rich mixture of face-to-face and/or e-learning activities
- use of different media, including text, audio or visual media
- opportunities for learners to exercise choice, e.g. of learning methods and/or activities
- alternative approaches to contacting and working with each other (both learner–trainer and learner–learner), including face-to-face sessions, e-mail and message systems, phone, Skype, online discussion groups.

Trainers frequently turn to blended learning as a means of capitalizing on the different and often complementary benefits of face-to-face learning activities and online learning. Commonly used online learning and teaching methods (see Chapter 4) include the use of:

- video clips and podcasts
- e-mail
- diagnostic tests and quizzes

- online assessment methods
- online guides
- social networking tools, e.g. online networking sites, tools such as Twitter
- blogs and wikis
- online telecommunications, e.g. Skype.

Blended learning also offers flexibility of time and space to both learners and tutors. For example, the time involved in physically attending a course can be reduced through the use of e-learning activities. Individuals can choose when they engage with their e-learning and select from a menu of opportunities to create an individualized learning experience that meets their needs and interests. One of the great advantages of blended learning is that it offers possibilities for new types of learning groups, e.g. multi-professional and/or international, that enable people to learn and work together across the traditional boundaries of time and place.

Design of blended learning programmes

The same design principles that are used for face-to-face and e-learning programmes are relevant to blended learning. This means that they require an aim or aims, learning outcomes and a logical structure, e.g. using the 4MAT method (see Chapter 5 and McCarthy, 2012). There are three main approaches to structuring blended learning programmes, which are illustrated in Figure 7.2 and outlined below:

- a core of face-to-face learning and teaching activities which are supported by e-learning activities and/or resources
- a core of online activities and resources which are supported by face-to-face activities
- alternatively, e-learning and face-to-face learning may be blended together in an integrated manner.

These different approaches are illustrated in the following case studies.

Case study 7.3 Blended learning programme – core of face-to-face learning and teaching activities

Martin is a research librarian working in a government library service. His customers are civil servants. Martin is required to teach his colleagues how to use specialist databases and he uses blended learning, as indicated in the following sequence of learning activities:

1 Advertises training event through in-house online communication methods.
2 Sends people who sign up for the course a welcoming e-mail and asks them to let him know about their current projects and information requirements.

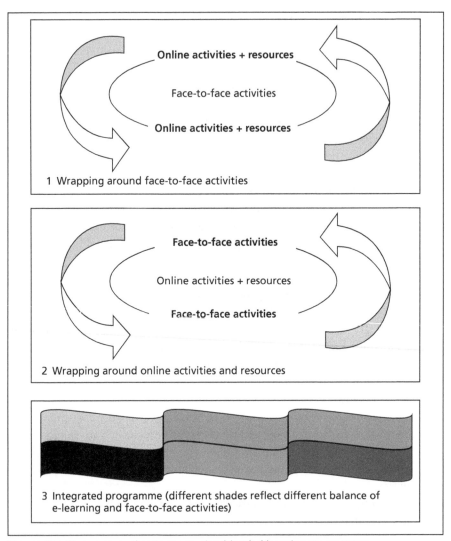

Figure 7.2 *Three approaches to structuring blended learning programmes*

3   Organizes a 30-minute training session in which he demonstrates the database.
4   After the training event, provides access to an online site with guides and Frequently
    Asked Questions. Colleagues are informed about this site via an e-mail.

Martin finds that this approach works. Previously, he ran three-hour training sessions but
attendance was poor and people often left after about an hour, citing pressure of work.
The new blended learning approach has resulted in larger numbers of people attending the
session and accessing the online resources.

Example 7.1 Blended learning – core of face-to-face learning and teaching activities

Sumona teaches information skills to first-year undergraduate students and has developed the following sequence of learning activities:

1 She sends an e-mail with access to a video clip to all students registered on the module. In the three-minute clip a third-year student talks about how the lecture helped him to find academic sources for his essays. He linked this to gaining good marks.

2 At the start of Sumona's lecture, one of the academics introduces the topic and stresses its importance to students' learning what is expected of them at university level.

3 During the lecture Sumona links the use of academic information sources to gaining a good quality degree. She uses a PowerPoint slide which links the gaining of different marks (more than 70%, 60–69%, 50–59%, 40–49% and less than 39%) to the use of academic literature.

4 She demonstrates three aspects of the library resources (e-books, databases and e-journals), using examples which are linked to the students' first assignment.

5 She ends the lecture by telling the students about additional resources which are available on their course module's VLE site.

6 Following the lecture, Sumona e-mails the students a short quiz, developed using SurveyMonkey. This helps them to assess their knowledge about information sources. It also serves as a reminder of the content of the lecture.

7 Finally, Sumona provides the students with access to her blog. She uses this to keep the students up to date.

Example 7.2 Outline structure for a blended learning course – core of online learning and teaching

Figure 7.3 provides an outline of a blended learning course which is based on online learning and teaching activities. The purpose of this course is to teach students how to reference their work. The course involves a range of activities including: reading e-mails, watching video clips, lecture, individual work, assignment, tutorial, and support via e-mail or phone.

Example 7.3 Outline structure for a blended learning induction session for new library assistants – integrated programme

Figure 7.4 illustrates an integrated blended learning programme for the induction of new library assistants. The programme involves e-learning via e-mail and online quizzes, as well as an online workshop activity. It also includes practical work in a library, as well as discussions and classroom-based activities.

Title of unit	Introduction to plagiarism						
Aim of unit	As a result of completing this training course, students will reference their work using the Harvard system						
Indicative learning outcomes	By the end of this unit, students will be able to: 1. Explain why referencing is important in academic work 2. Reference their work using the Harvard system						
Days	Topic	Type of activity	Tutor activity	Student activity	Student time	Informal assessment activities	Resources
Day 1	Awareness raising	Online	Send introductory e-mail to all students. E-mail contains link to a video clip in which a final-year student talks about the importance of referencing	Receive e-mail advising them of importance of lecture and the number of students who are caught plagiarizing each year	5 min	None	Text for e-mail Plagiarism statistics Video clip 1 Transcript of video clip
Day 2	Introduction to plagiarism and referencing	Lecture	Lecture	Listen to lecture Take part in plagiarism quiz activity	50 min	Results of quiz	Lecture notes Quiz Handout
Day 2	The students' experience	Online	E-mail link to second video clip with interviews of students and academic staff talking about their experiences of referencing	Watch video clip Contribute to online discussion	2 h	Evidence of postings	Text for activity Video clip 2 Transcript of video clip
Days 3–5	Correct referencing	Solo	Send e-mail asking students to bring draft assignment to tutorial	Prepare and bring draft assignment to tutorial	2 h	Will bring to tutorial	Text for activity
Days 3–5	Correct referencing	Small group tutorial	Facilitate tutorial	Assess each other's use of referencing	50 min	Feedback to each other	Handout
Day 1 onwards	Help	Online	Remind students of your availability for help – e-mail, phone	Use tutor help facility	Various	Evidence of postings or e-mails	Text for activity Handout

Figure 7.3 *Example blended learning programme on plagiarism*

Title of unit	Introduction to the layout of the City Public Library for new library assistants					
Aim of unit	As a result of completing this event, new colleagues will be able to find their way around the library					
Indicative learning outcomes	By the end of this unit, colleagues will be able to: 1. Find their way around the physical and virtual public library 2. Guide readers to relevant departments or sections within the library.					
Topic	Type of activity	Tutor activity	Participant activity	Student time	Informal assessment activities	Resources
1 Welcome	Individual	Send e-mail with link to video clip	Read e-mail and watch video clip	10 min	None	Text for e-mail Video clip
2 Introduction	Classroom	Introduction and welcome. Give out folder	Introduce selves Collect folder Listen	20 min	None	Folder
3 Finding your way around the library – quiz	Pairs – library based	Introduce activity	In pairs, work through quiz by walking around the library and answering questions	30 min	Results of quiz	Floor plan Handout
4 De-briefing activity	Classroom	Facilitate de-briefing session Answer questions	Listen, question and answer Contribute to discussion	15 min	Observe language used in discussions	
5 Website	Pairs - online	Introduce activity	In pairs work through quiz by searching through website	30 min	Results of quiz	Answer sheet
6 De-briefing activity	Classroom	Facilitate de-briefing session Answer questions	Listen, question and answer Contribute to discussion	10 min	Questions and answers	Answer sheet
7 Question and answer session. Summary	Classroom	Facilitate de-briefing session Answer questions	Listen, question and answer Contribute to discussion	10 min	Questions and answers	
8 Follow-up 'extension' quiz	Online	E-mail a new quiz to participants	Complete quiz	30 min	Results of quiz	Text for activity Quiz
9 Close session	Online	E-mail colleagues with answers and thank them for their participation	Read e-mail	2–3 min	Not applicable	Text plus answers

Figure 7.4 *Blended induction session for new library assistants*

TIP FOR TRAINERS

If you are developing a blended learning course, then imagine yourself in different roles, e.g. as tutor and as a participant, and work through the plan thinking about it from their different perspectives. Ask yourself whether the course works in terms of participants achieving the learning outcomes and having an excellent learning experience. ■

E-tutoring

E-tutoring is a day-to-day activity for most library and information workers as they respond to e-mails requesting help and advice. Leading and facilitating e-learning or blended learning programmes is an extension of this activity and requires a similar skill-set.

Early research by Collins and Berge (1996) identified the following four main types of e-tutoring activities:

- Pedagogical activities involve designing appropriate online programmes and learning activities and guiding the learner(s) through the learning process. This means that the e-tutor needs the necessary subject knowledge as well as skills in facilitating learning, such as: answering queries, leading discussions, setting up and running online activities.
- Social activities are important in e-learning and blended learning and these include creating a friendly and informal environment; helping individuals to introduce themselves and establish an online presence; acknowledging learners' contributions and encouraging teamwork. This is the second stage of the six-stage model of e-learning (see earlier in this chapter) and it provides the 'glue' that helps individuals to work together as an online group.
- Managing the learning process involves starting the online course and facilitating introductions; introducing the course; setting the pace; introducing and setting tasks; focusing and refocusing the discussion or online conference; managing the time; summarizing the outcomes; closing the discussion or conference. The learning group may be led by an e-tutor whose style is directive, or by someone with a 'light touch'.
- Managing the technology involves knowing how to use the technology which supports the online programme and being able to access technical back-up from either the tutor's own organization or their supplier.

Online learning and teaching involve e-tutors (and learners) in developing new skills. The practical realities of learning online include the need to:

- develop an online voice
- manage time for online activities
- develop skills in reading and following threads
- develop skills in engaging learners in online activities.

Developing an online voice means finding a style of writing to participants in an online environment where there may be no visual cues for the e-learner, and is a method of projecting yourself and your professional image. One approach to developing your online presence is to use 'softeners' or sentences which help the reader to see you as a friendly and accessible tutor.

There is concern about information- and work-overload in e-tutors. It can be quite a challenge to return to work after a weekend and discover 60–100 new messages in the e-learning site as well as your own e-mails. It is really important for new e-tutors to be clear about the demands and expectations that arise from this role. The following strategies are useful for managing time in a virtual environment:

- Set very clear boundaries around time online.
- Let learners know how often you are likely to be online, e.g. three to four times a week.
- Reply to individual e-mails with an open e-mail or discussion group message to the whole group (edit out personal information as appropriate).
- Set up a frequently asked questions (FAQs) list.

It is a great advantage to have speed-reading skills and to be able to skim quickly through a large number of messages and make sense of them. Some strategies for managing conversations online include:

- establishing ground rules about one topic per discussion group message or e-mail
- asking participants for volunteers to summarize key points or discussions
- checking with the participants that you have not missed any important points.

How do you engage students or end-users in online activities? In general, individuals will participate in online activities if they are comfortable in the online environment and can see the benefit of the activity to themselves. Some strategies for engaging e-learners include:

- using the six-step model (see earlier in this chapter)
- using relevant and authentic materials, e.g. real-life case studies or problems based on the e-learners' own situations
- bringing in a new stimulus (as in face-to-face sessions), e.g. a virtual visitor or a relevant video clip, if an online process is flagging
- asking the e-learners for their feedback. They may be ready to move on to the next stage of the course!

As in face-to-face training courses, e-tutors are likely to experience difficult situations. Examples include:

- flaming (the online equivalent of road rage)
- quiet students or non-participants (sometimes called 'browsers' or 'lurkers')
- dominant students
- online work fizzling out.

When faced with a difficult situation e-tutors need to consider:

1 whether or not to intervene
2 when to intervene
3 how to intervene – what organizational policies and procedures need to be taken into account?
4 how to intervene – in group or in private. If in private, then is it best to do by e-mail, by phone or face-to-face?
5 the likely short- and long-term implications of the intervention – for the individuals, for the whole group and for the e-tutor
6 whether or not to get help or support, e.g. from a colleague or specialist such as a disabilities officer.

TIP FOR TRAINERS

When sending an e-mail to an e-learner in response to a tricky situation, check for unintended consequences. Is it possible for your e-mail to be misread or misinterpreted? Does it need to be phrased more clearly? Have you sent 'soft' messages or 'hard' messages? How would you like to receive such an e-mail? ■

Evaluation of e-learning and blended learning

The evaluation principles introduced in Chapter 5 are relevant to e-learning and blended learning, and this means that trainers can use the four levels of the Kirkpatrick (1994) model to evaluate training:

- reaction of student – what they thought and felt about the training
- learning – what they learnt as a result of the training
- behaviour – what impact the training has had on their behaviour, e.g. at work or in their educational course
- impact – the effect of the training on the library and information service, and on the parent organization.

The particular evaluation methods associated with each level are outlined in Chapter 5, Table 5.7.

E-learning and blended learning raise some additional issues in terms of evaluation. In addition to the ideas introduced in Chapter 5, trainers need to evaluate the online environment and the e-learning resources. The following questions can be used in this process.

Online environment:

1 Is the learning environment easy to access?
2 Do security systems work without being too cumbersome?
3 Is the structure and layout of the learning environment intuitive?

4 Is the design of the environment attractive and visually pleasing?
5 Is it possible to take different routes through the learning environment?
6 Do all facilities work, e.g. links, quizzes, surveys?
7 Does it meet the required accessibility standards?
8 Does it work on a range of different devices and operating systems?

E-learning resources:

1 Is there a variety of learning resources which involve the use of a range of senses such as sight, sound?
2 Are they easy to access and quick to download?
3 Is there a clear statement of aims, learning outcomes or objectives?
4 Do the resources arouse the learner's interest?
5 Do they use clear language?
6 Is the content organized into manageable chunks?
7 Is the content relevant?
8 Is the content up to date?
9 Is there a variety of routes through the materials?
10 Do the resources use supporting images and diagrams?
11 Are there opportunities for learners to practise, e.g. activities and quizzes?
12 Is personalized feedback provided?
13 Are the resources up to date?

Summary

This chapter has brought together a range of ideas relating to e-learning and blended learning courses. These are in addition to ideas explored in the earlier chapters. In essence, web-based tutorials require the designer to provide online equivalents to the stages of learning that are likely to be experienced in face-to-face situations, and they need to mitigate for the absence of a trainer.

Trainers involved in establishing e-learning groups and communities need to develop learning processes which enable individuals to participate in group and community learning activities. A model based on the work of Gilly Salmon (2000) has been presented in this chapter, and this provides a framework for the development of learner and trainer activities.

Blended learning provides trainers with an opportunity to combine the benefits of both face-to-face and e-learning. Learning and teaching methods and technologies introduced in Chapters 3 and 4 can be used to develop engaging blended learning training programmes. The section on design provided some practical examples of different types of blended learning programme.

Finally, the section on evaluation considered the application to e-learning and blended learning courses of ideas first introduced in Chapter 5. In addition to the traditional methods of evaluating training courses, it is important to evaluate the virtual environment and the online learning resources. This enables the added, online dimension of the training event to be evaluated.

References and additional resources

Collins, M. and Berge, Z. (1996) Facilitating Interaction In Computer Mediated On-line Courses, *FSU/AECT Distance Education Conference: Proceedings*, Tallahassee, June.

Elston, C. and Schneider, M. (2011) Library Induction: online vs face-to face, *SCONUL Focus*, **52**, 31–4.

Herrington, J., Reeves, T. C. and Oliver, R. (2009) *A Guide to Authentic E-learning*, Routledge.

Iverson, K. (2004) *E-learning Games*, Pearson.

Kear, K. (2010) *Online and Social Networking Communities*, Routledge.

Kirkpatrick, D. L. (1994) *Evaluating Training Programs*, Berrett-Koehler Publishers.

Ko, S. and Rossen, S. (2010) *Teaching Online. A practical guide*, 3rd edn, Routledge.

McCarthy, B. (2012) *The 4MAT Approach to Training*, www.aboutlearning.com/ [accessed on 12 August 2012].

Moust, J., Bouhuijs, P. and Schmidt, H. (2007) *Introduction to Problem-based Learning*, Routledge.

Nelson, B. C. and Erlandson, B. E. (2012) *Design for Learning in Virtual Worlds*, Routledge.

Pacansky-Brock, M. (2012) *Best Practices for Teaching with Emerging Technologies*, Routledge.

Salmon, G. (2000) *E-moderating: the key to teaching and learning online*, Kogan Page.

Salmon, G. (2002) *E-tivities: the key to active online learning*, Routledge.

Salmon, G. (2011) *E-moderating: the key to online teaching and learning*, 3rd edn, Routledge.

Savin-Baden, M. (2007) *A Practical Guide to Problem-based Learning Online*, Routledge.

Thomas, M. (ed.) (2011) *Deconstructing Digital Natives: young people, technology, and the new literacies*, Routledge.

Vai, M. and Sosulski, K. (2011) *Essentials of Online Course Design*, Routledge.

Part 2

Learning in the workplace

8

Learning and development in the workplace

Introduction

This chapter provides a brief introduction to over 90 ideas for workplace learning. Many of these ideas may be used either as part of a training programme or as standalone activities to promote individual or team learning. The chapter does not include any tips for trainers, as its aim is to provide a general overview of different approaches to learning and development in the workplace.

The concept of workplace learning received a boost through the rise in popularity of the 70:20:10 model of development, which is described in Chapter 2. The basic idea behind the 70:20:10 framework is that 70% of learning takes place in the workplace through dealing with challenging activities; 20% of learning involves learning from colleagues; and 10% is based on courses and reading.

The topics in this chapter are organized alphabetically and provide busy trainers and managers with more than 90 ideas for workplace learning. Where appropriate, ideas are cross-referenced to relevant chapters earlier in the book.

Many of the ideas presented here are relevant to trainers who want to keep their knowledge and skills up to date. My own approach is to read professional journals, keep an eye on my favourite blogs (see Blogs below), attend an occasional conference (often online) or webinar, engage in challenging projects and talk to practitioners and delegates who attend my training events.

Example 8.1 Keeping training relevant and up to date – the perspective of an independent trainer

As an external trainer, I always want my training to be up to date and relevant. I have a number of ways in which I keep abreast of changing training needs, and of research and other factors that impact on the content of courses. I regularly speak to practitioners working in the library and education fields. I subscribe to a number of online and print journals, and keep an eye on a range of blogs. Email-based discussion forums, Twitter and Facebook alert me to current concerns, new issues and research. When I am planning training I spend a lot of time talking with the training organiser

about needs within the organisation. Comments by delegates during courses often
alert me to new issues.

Harding (2012)

90+ APPROACHES TO LEARNING AND DEVELOPMENT IN THE WORKPLACE

360 degree feedback

360 degree feedback is a process which is often incorporated into management and leadership development programmes, and also into appraisal processes. It is called 360 degree feedback because the circle of people around someone at work have an opportunity to provide feedback. The basic idea is that someone asks different groups of people to provide them with feedback privately, via a structured questionnaire which is often managed online. Typically, they may ask their line manager, peers and individuals in their team for feedback. This feedback may well be clustered around themes such as ability to work in a team; communication skills; learning and development in the workplace. Individuals may be asked to score their colleague and then provide written feedback. All of the feedback is then collated, e.g. by a staff development officer, and then presented to the person at the centre of the process. This is normally done face-to-face, in the context of a supportive development meeting.

Accreditations

External accreditations bodies such as Investors in People or CustomerFirstUK provide an opportunity for library and information services to develop and demonstrate their quality. Typically, gaining an external accreditation involves:

- benchmarking your service and/or processes against a standard
- identifying any gaps
- working through a development process to enable you to meet the standard
- demonstrating that you meet the required standard.

The benefits of external accreditations include:

- improvement and demonstration of quality of services and activities
- improved internal systems and processes
- opportunity to take part in a structured development process with external support
- opportunity for a team-building and organizational-development process
- opportunity for external recognition.

Example 8.2 Investors in People

Writing in 2008 about the Investors in People Award, Dr Paul Ayris, Director of Library Services at University College London, said: 'As Head of Department, I am delighted for all members of UCL library staff who participated in gaining this award. It's a tribute to their dedication, professionalism and the quality of the contribution they make to the success of UCL.' Working towards the Investors in People Award included a comprehensive staff development process as well as developing communication processes through committee structures and user surveys, and introducing KPIs.

Action learning

Action learning is a process which involves a small group of people coming together and working on a particular problem or live issue (see for example Pedler, 1996). The group may be self-organizing or led by a facilitator. The advantages and disadvantages are outlined in Table 8.1.

Table 8.1 *Advantages and disadvantages of action learning*

Advantages	Disadvantages
Sharing of expertise and insights	May be time consuming
Introduction to a new approach to problem solving	Action-learning group may not be productive
Development of problem-solving skills and experience	Suits particular types of problems, e.g. complex, medium- or long-term problems
Development of skills and experience in reflective practice	Solution(s) will depend on capabilities of group members, which may be limited

Action learning is real-life learning on real problems which may be complex and messy. An important aspect of action learning is that it is a structured process which involves reflection and learning from reflection. It involves a number of stages:

1 formation of the group
2 deciding on working practices for the group (how often it will meet, who will facilitate, etc.)
3 identifying problem(s) to be addressed
4 working on problems, and at the same time reflecting on the process and on the results
5 developing solutions
6 reflecting on the overall process and outcomes.

Case study 8.1 Action learning

As part of her leadership development programme organized by her employer (a university), Jane had the opportunity to join an action learning group made up of four other managers from across the institution. Over a period of six months the group met every four weeks for three to four hours. Its sessions were facilitated by an external facilitator. Jane used this opportunity to obtain help and support and to reflect on a change management process which involved restructuring within the library and information service. When she was asked about this experience, she said that it helped to give her confidence to lead her part of the change process, that she gained new ideas and perspectives from her peers and that it led to important and very strong links with colleagues in other parts of the university.

Action planning
See Chapter 3.

Analysing mistakes
Mistakes provide good opportunities for learning. It is worthwhile developing a blame-free culture, as this will enable individuals to share their mistakes and learn from them. Alternatively, in organizations where there is a culture of blaming individuals who make mistakes, these may be hidden, covered up or rationalized. This will limit opportunities for learning and may also lead to greater problems.

There are a number of approaches to making sure that learning from mistakes is built into everyday activities:

1 Managers and leaders need to be open about the mistakes that they make and discuss them as learning opportunities.
2 Include learning from mistakes on the agenda of team meetings and ensure that these are discussed in a constructive and blame-free manner, with a focus on learning.
3 At the end of projects or other activities ask 'What can we learn from this experience?' or 'If we repeat this, can we improve it?'.

Appraisal processes
Appraisal meetings provide a useful opportunity for learning from feedback. Ideally, they provide time and space for reflection and for thinking about how to improve performance. Most organizations have their own internal appraisal process, and staff are supported by appraisal training. Sadly, too often the focus of an appraisal process is on completing the paperwork or reports on an online system rather than on its being a learning process.

A typical appraisal process involves:

• preparation for the meeting
• the actual meeting
• agreement about the outcomes of the meeting
• follow-up meetings.

Preparation for an appraisal meeting may involve the following activities:

- Appraisee:
  — reflection on current performance and future development plans, completion of associated documentation
  — agreement on meeting time and place.
- Appraiser:
  — reading the documents and considering how to provide feedback and identify areas for development
  — identification of a suitable time and place (quiet location without interruptions).

The actual appraisal meeting is likely to involve the following activities:

- review of current performance – successes, strengths and areas for development
- identification of performance targets (often called KPIs)
- identification of personal development action plan.

Both parties then need to agree a written summary of the meeting, including the action plan, and then this is signed off. Follow-up meetings then take place, e.g. at monthly or bi-monthly intervals, as this gives an opportunity to monitor progress and provide advice and support as required.

Apps

An app (or application software) provides an opportunity for disseminating information, an online training process or learning resources to a smartphone, laptop, tablet or other appropriate electronic device. Apps are described in more detail in Chapter 4.

Asking advice

Asking advice is an important means of learning from colleagues or customers. It is empowering, as it enables someone to share their experience or expertise, and so validates and values them. Asking advice encourages the other person to:

- reflect on their own experience
- summarize that experience
- present it.

Sometimes, asking for advice produces unexpected results, as is illustrated in the following two case studies.

Case study 8.2 Use of ice-breakers

Nihal, a library trainer, was preparing a training session in her company for a group of staff who had a reputation for being difficult. She asked a colleague, Nick, a marketing consultant, if she could run through the training programme with him. Nick thought the overall programme was very good but was concerned about Nihal's introduction of an ice-breaker at the start of the event. Nihal explained that this would help to relax everyone and help them to work together. Nick's advice was that these people knew each other very well and that an ice-breaker might irritate them. He suggested that it be omitted and that Nihal use a challenging database search exercise instead – this would focus people's attention and demonstrate the importance of the course. Nihal followed Nick's advice and the course worked well.

Case study 8.3 Talking in the library

Thomas worked in a college library. The library team was finding it difficult to manage behaviours in the reading room. Students were noisy and disrespectful of each other and also some of the library staff, who regularly received complaints about this issue. Thomas and his team tried a number of different methods to improve the situation, but none worked.

Thomas called a meeting of the student representatives and asked for their help in managing the problem. The students decided to design a poster reminding students of the required behaviours, and they offered to monitor behaviours within the library on a rota basis. Thomas arranged for them to receive a one-hour training session and they then began their duties. Immediately the level of noise and unacceptable behaviours dropped. If situations arose where the student helper needed support, they would come to Thomas and his team for help. Very quickly the atmosphere in the library changed. The student helpers decided that they wanted to be called 'Library Ambassadors' and met regularly with the library staff to give their input on different topics. At the end of the year Thomas invited them all to attend a 'thank you' meal at which they were each given a £50 book token.

Asking and answering questions

Questions are a powerful tool for learning in the workplace. They can be used to:

- acquire information or ideas
- obtain a reaction or test ideas
- get clarification
- understand something from another person's perspective.

Questions can also be used as a means of balancing one's own thinking processes. For example, if someone thinks and talks about an issue at a very general level, then use questions to shift their focus to a more detailed level. Sometimes, when exploring a problem it is useful to use questions as a means to understand the issue from different people's perspectives, e.g. a customer, a library assistant, a professional librarian, an IT manager.

It is sometimes useful to preface questions with 'a softener', as this helps to make the process more conversational and less potentially challenging. For example:

- 'I'm not sure that I understand this … do you mind explaining …'
- 'I'm concerned about … How do you think we should move forward …?'
- 'I may be missing the point here, but I …'

Finally, some extremely powerful questions which may be used in lots of different situations are:

- 'What can we learn from it?'
- 'How can we improve it next time around?'
- 'If you were advising a new member of staff on this topic, what advice would you give?'

Audio recordings

Audio recordings have the advantage of being relatively inexpensive and requiring unsophisticated technologies. They can be listened to in the workplace, while travelling or at home. There are two main ways in which audio recordings can be used as a focus of workplace learning. First, recordings of speeches, presentations, articles or selections from books can be used as a complement to training and development programmes. There are many different sources for recordings, including iTunes. Second, audio recording can be used as a tool for reflection and workplace learning. It doesn't require sophisticated equipment, e.g. many mobile phones have this facility. Examples of this type of application include recording meetings or customer service interventions, playing back the recording and reflecting on it. Clearly, the people involved in this activity need to give their full consent.

See also Podcasts in Chapter 4.

Benchmarking

Benchmarking involves comparing an aspect of a library and information service, or indeed the whole service, with another service. It is a useful means of learning from peers and obtaining ideas for improving performance and development. However, it can be time consuming. Typically, a benchmarking activity involves:

- positioning the library and information service in the context of a group of peer services
- identifying services equivalent to yours
- identifying library and information services you aspire to
- identifying areas to be benchmarked
- selecting a benchmarking partner

- obtaining permission from the benchmarking partner
- agreeing to the benchmarking process
- completing the benchmarking process
- reporting on the outcomes of benchmarking
- deciding on subsequent actions.

Case study 8.4 Benchmarking voluntary organizations' websites

Daphne worked for a small voluntary organization which provided a range of services to people with disabilities. Her role was to develop the library and information services. When she started working for the organization she thought the information aspects of the website were weak but she wasn't sure how to proceed. She decided to complete a benchmarking project and identified five national voluntary organizations and ten small voluntary organizations with similar remits to her own. She worked through their websites and produced a report which identified typical features of a good-quality website and 'nice to have' facilities. She also visited one of the organizations and talked with its research officer (who had responsibility for the library) about his experience. Daphne used the results to produce a website development strategy which she presented to her manager.

Case study 8.5 A holiday in the Netherlands

Margaret worked in a public library in the UK and had special responsibility for the children's library. While she was on holiday in the Netherlands she noticed a public library and walked into it. She wandered around the library noting different ideas which she could take home with her. A librarian asked if she could help, and Margaret explained that she was on holiday and had come in out of interest. She was then given a full tour of the library and had coffee with a group of library workers, during which they exchanged ideas. Margaret took photos of the library and some of the displays, which she took back to her own library, where she shared ideas with her colleagues.

Blogs

A blog or weblog is a web-based tool which enables individuals to write about and share ideas, experiences and links with colleagues and/or customers. Both writing and reading a blog provides opportunities for learning. Blogs are described in more detail in Chapter 4.

Book reviews

Writing and reading book reviews are good methods of updating one's knowledge. Professional bodies, specialist groups and professional journals may want the services of a book reviewer at some stage. One of the advantages is that you get to keep the book! Within an individual service, colleagues can arrange to update each other's knowledge by reviewing a book, e.g. on management and leadership, team supervision, library and information work, information technology, and then share the review with colleagues either orally or in writing.

Briefing papers

Producing a briefing paper, e.g. a one-page summary, is a useful technique for helping staff to present a topic and its key issues. Both the author and the reader will benefit from a briefing paper. Examples of typical topics for briefing papers include the following:

- new system or procedure
- new resource
- an article, book or report
- visit to another library
- a conference
- a training event.

Example 8.3 Conference feedback

In a university library and information service it is normal practice for a member of staff who has attended an external event to write a briefing paper of no more than one side of A4. These are then posted to the library staff portal, and accessed via a link from the weekly staff e-bulletin.

Briefing sessions

As its name suggests, a briefing session is a short event, often involving a presentation which provides a summary, e.g. of a forthcoming change, new service or resource. Both leading and attending briefing sessions are occasions for learning. Sometimes establishing a tight boundary, e.g. in terms of time frame, number of PowerPoint slides or length of document, helps to focus the session, and also the learning that takes place.

Cascade training

This involves individuals in sharing their learning, e.g. one person shares their learning with two others, who then each share it with another pair. The advantages of cascade training are that it helps to promote team learning and it can help the transmission of important messages across the library service. However, there is potential for misinformation and for the dilution of the original message.

Celebrating success

Celebrating success is an important aspect of acknowledging achievements, hard work and learning. The benefits are that celebrations are motivating events, send a strong message about what is valued within a library and information service and provide an opportunity for reflection. Their cost in terms of time and other resources can be accommodated to suit the situation. Celebrations can be relatively small, e.g. a few cakes, or a large party.

Coaching

Coaching is a method of helping individuals to improve their performance. The concept of coaching is widely used in the worlds of sports and of the performing arts. It is also very relevant to training practice and can be used to help individuals develop their skills, e.g. in online searching or in using specific tools such as EndNote or RefWorks.

Coaching sessions can be organized in a number of different ways. The simplest approach to running a coaching session involves the following stages:

1 Agree on the learning outcome for the session.
2 Briefly discuss the benefits of achieving the learning outcome (this may take only a minute).
3 Explain the technique or topic.
4 Let the trainee practise the technique or topic.
5 Ask if there are any questions.
6 Assess whether or not the trainee has achieved the learning outcome.
7 End the session with a brief summary and thank the trainee for their work.

Advantages of coaching sessions:

• One-to-one learning activity is focused on the specific needs of the learner.
• Learning is embedded in reality, e.g. the workplace.
• The coach can be flexible and meet the specific needs of the learner.
• Sessions can be short or long and can be fitted in with everyday work activities.

Disadvantages of coaching sessions:

• They require a skilled coach.
• In a few organizations they have a bad reputation and are seen as a 'remedial' activity.

Case study 8.6 Managing poor performance

Paul is the team leader of a group of customer service assistants whose main role is shelving books. He is a relatively inexperienced manager but has completed a staff development programme on 'leading your team'. Paul is still uncertain about how to tackle performance issues and has a member of staff who consistently shelves books inaccurately. Paul works with a coach from the Human Resources department. The structure of his session is set out in Table 8.2.

Table 8.2 *Example coaching session structure*

Structure of the coaching session	Example content
1 Agree learning outcome for the session	Agreed learning outcome is 'To enable Paul to manage a meeting with the member of staff who consistently shelves books inaccurately'.
2 Briefly discuss the benefits of achieving this learning outcome (this may take only a minute)	The coach and Paul agree that if he could tackle this issue effectively then it would: • improve the quality of work produced by this member of staff • help Paul to be more confident about tackling such issues in the future.
3 Explain the technique or topic	The coach provides Paul with a specific strategy for meeting with the member of staff and structuring the conversation.
4 Let the trainee practise the technique or topic	Paul practises the technique, as a role play activity, with the coach playing the part of the member of staff. He repeats this three times until both Paul and the coach are satisfied with the result.
5 Ask if there are any questions	Paul asks the coach for his advice on what to do if the member of staff responds in a number of different ways. They then discuss different strategies for dealing with this.
6 Assess whether or not the trainee has achieved the learning outcome	The coach assesses that Paul has the right skills and a clear plan for dealing with the situation.
7 End the session with a brief summary and thank the trainee for their work	The session ends with Paul and the coach thanking each other. They agree to a follow-up session within a week of Paul's holding his meeting with the member of staff.

Case study 8.7 Supervising a team

Janine had recently become a new team supervisor in a public library. She found it very challenging to deal with difficult situations, particularly as she felt that many of her team members were her friends – they had worked together for many years. She felt that some people were taking advantage of her, e.g. by arriving late and by taking long lunch breaks. She explained this to her line manager, who arranged for her to attend the local authority's two-day Supervision training. This was augmented by one-to-one coaching. Janine attended six coaching sessions and these enabled her to develop a structure and approach for dealing with difficult situations. She role-played particular situations with her coach and found that this gave her the confidence that she needed in order to tackle the real-life situations. After four months in her new role, Janine felt that she was beginning to learn how to deal with all staff in an equitable and fair manner, and she felt much more confident about tackling challenging situations.

Communities of interest and practice

The concept of communities of interest and practice came from the work of Wenger, McDermott and Snyder (2002). A community of interest is a group of people who come together to share information, ideas and experiences relating to a particular topic, e.g. use of Kindles, use of blogs in training. Typically, communities of interest may have very large memberships, up to 1000+. In contrast, communities of practice are relatively small groups whose focus is often a particular aspect of professional development or practice, e.g. an action learning set, or group established to work on a problem experienced by a number of information services. Joining a community of interest or a community of practice is a useful means of engaging with professional networks either at a very general level (community of interest) or in a very focused way (community of practice).

Competitions and prizes

Internal and external competitions and prizes are a useful means of focusing energy and action on a specific goal. They can be extremely motivating and can be used as an occasion to showcase achievements or as a staff development opportunity. They provide individuals or teams with an opportunity to:

- gain recognition for their knowledge, skills or expertise
- gain validation for their work
- develop new skills, e.g. making an application for an award, etc.
- present themselves as possible role models.

Entering for a competition or prize requires a range of skills, including:

- goal setting
- developing a strategy
- producing a statement (or multimedia output) which meets defined requirements
- working with feedback from colleagues in the preparation stages
- managing the outcome, e.g. success or failure.

Competitions are regularly advertised in the professional literature and they may focus on: a particular sector, e.g. school libraries; specific types of activities or resources, e.g. marketing or public relations; particular groups of staff, e.g. early-career professionals, staff living and working in a particular country or region. Library and information workers may also apply for competitions and prizes outside of their profession, e.g. local authorities sometimes organize customer service awards; individual sectors offer prizes, e.g. the Higher Education Academy runs the National Teaching Fellowship awards; special interest groups make awards, e.g. for services to a particular group such as people with disabilities, young carers or homeless people.

Example 8.4 Travelling Librarian's Award

The English-Speaking Union and the Chartered Institute of Library and Information Professionals offer an annual Travelling Librarian's Award, which provides an opportunity for an individual to travel and learn about library and information practices in another country or countries. The recipient of the award is required to submit a written report and also to maintain a blog to enable other librarians to follow their travels.

Complaints

Complaints provide vital feedback on failures or weaknesses in library and information services. They can be used to promote learning and development as:

- case studies for discussion in training events
- foci for reflection and discussion in staff meetings
- indicators of the need for staff training.

Conferences

Professional conferences provide excellent opportunities for networking and for learning from peers. They also provide great opportunities for developing presentation skills, networking skills and, if you are on the organizing committee, project management skills. Conferences vary hugely in terms of their costs and time commitments. Increasingly, online conferences offer a relatively cheap and convenient alternative to attending a traditional conference.

How to make the most of conferences:

- Get involved in their organization.
- Offer to present a paper or poster.
- Offer to run a workshop.
- Offer to write the conference blog (see Chapter 5).
- Read all the advance information and identify people and sessions to attend.
- Network while you are there (see Networking).
- Write a summary report of your experience – for your colleagues, an in-house e-bulletin, or a professional journal or website.
- Brief your colleagues about your experience (see Briefing papers).

Covering for holidays

Covering all or part of the work of a colleague is a useful way of gaining new experience or trying out a new role. There are many different approaches to arranging holiday cover and they include:

- dividing a particular role into specific tasks and activities and sharing these out amongst a team
- letting the team members take responsibility for sharing out the tasks and activities amongst themselves
- using it as an occasion to provide someone with an opportunity to 'step up' and add to their experience

- delegating part of the cover upward, i.e. giving a team leader or manager the opportunity to learn about the operational detail of one aspect of the work.

Case study 8.8 Holiday cover in a small voluntary organization

Chuka runs a small library in a sports organization and he is the sole librarian. He planned cover for his one-month holiday as follows:

- Two volunteers would be trained up to deal with administrative work.
- A library school student would provide additional support and deal with all queries. This was on a paid basis.
- Chuka's manager would meet with the student on a weekly basis to monitor the situation and provide support.

Crises

Crises do occur in the workplace, as the result of: a sudden change in legislation; disasters such as fire or floods; war, civil unrest or terrorism; serious incidents; or changes in the parent organization, e.g. merger, financial crisis, technology crises. They do provide learning opportunities (however painful) and they give rise to a series of activities both in terms of the immediate and long-term responses. Preparing for such a situation will make it easier to manage if it should happen. This involves developing emergency response plans which include clear procedures for decision making at different levels.

Case study 8.9 Refurbishment of a college library

The top floor of a further education college library was closed for refurbishment over the summer. It was due to be handed back two weeks before the start of term. Towards the end of the building work, the project team discovered asbestos, which meant that the refurbishment would not be completed until four weeks after the start of term. The college's senior managers and library staff quickly developed a plan which enabled them to provide a skeleton service for the first few weeks of term, including a temporary reading room in another building.

Once the builders had completed their work and the library was up and running as normal, they reflected on their experience by answering the following questions:

- Why had the crisis occurred?
- What had it involved?
- How had it developed?
- How had it been resolved?
- What could be learnt from the experience – by the librarian and library staff, the senior management team and the building contractors?

Critical friend

A critical friend could be a colleague from your own library or information service or from another service. Their role is to provide an external perspective. They are particularly useful when developing a new service or activity, when there is low turnover of staff (and therefore little input of new ideas) or if you want external validation for a particular activity.

Case study 8.10 Developing a new marketing strategy

A university library was developing a new marketing strategy and organized a half-day workshop involving leaders and managers from the library and the university's marketing manager. A colleague from another university library who had extensive experience of marketing was invited to attend the workshop as a critical friend. The critical friend's role was to input her knowledge and experience, provide an external perspective and be constructively critical of the outcomes of the day. She did this by engaging with the workshop activities, providing oral feedback on the workshop at the end of the day and writing a brief report on the workshop and its outcomes. The librarian was pleased with the outcomes of the workshop and recognized the value of involving a critical friend.

Delegation

Delegation brings different opportunities for both the person delegating the activity or task and the one who has agreed to carry it out. The person doing the delegating has the opportunity to:

- learn about successful approaches to delegation
- learn about management, authority and responsibility
- learn from the debriefing, e.g. operational issues or new ways of handling a task
- save time for other activities
- improve their job satisfaction.

The person who completes the task has the opportunity to:

- develop their knowledge and skills
- gain new insights into the library and information service
- improve their job satisfaction
- strengthen their curriculum vitae.

As with any process, there needs to be clarity about the delegation process and what is expected by each party. Different people have different approaches to delegation, which may involve:

- the whole task being delegated and the person delegating it being interested

only in the task's being completed to the required standard
- the whole task being delegated but the person delegating it loosely monitoring the process and outcomes
- the whole task being delegated but the person delegating it closely monitoring the process and outcomes.

Misunderstandings about delegation and the delegation process can be a cause of friction in the workplace.

Case study 8.11 Running a training event

Martin, an information officer, delegated the running of a training event to a graduate intern, Trino. Martin outlined what he required and explained the process and provided supporting documentation. He then let Trino get on with the task but met with him at weekly intervals to review it. This process worked well and the training event was a success. On their feedback forms, a number of delegates commented on Trino's helpfulness. Martin was pleased, as it gave him more time to work on other activities. Trino enjoyed the training event and was pleased that the experience had enhanced his curriculum vitae.

Demonstrations

Demonstrations are commonly used as a training method for teaching people how to use a particular database or other resource, or a system. These are described in Chapter 4.

Another type of demonstration is to role-play 'good and bad' practice, e.g. answering the phone or dealing with a customer. This can be a fun type of staff training and involves:

- working in pairs or trios
- each pair or trio choosing a particular topic to demonstrate
- time to prepare (say, ten minutes)
- each pair or trio demonstrating first the bad and then the good practice to the whole group.

For some reason, this type of activity works very well and generates a lot of laughter. Although it is a form of role play it is probably best not to use this term, as some people have strong negative feelings about role play.

Diaries

See Learning journals.

Displays

Producing and looking at library displays is a useful way of motivating people to learn. A quick search of the internet shows that there are many websites that share ideas for library displays. 'Library Displays' an engaging blog by a school librarian working in New Zealand provides many ideas for school and other librarians.[1]

Examples of library displays focused on staff development and learning include:

- Top ten training tips
- Challenging customers and how to deal with them
- Using ... [a particular database]
- A day in the life of ...

E-bulletins

Writing and producing an e-bulletin provides learning opportunities for both the people producing it and the reader. It is possible to produce an e-bulletin relatively simply using standard newsletter or e-bulletin templates provided by software suppliers such as Microsoft or available free from a variety of internet sources.

It is important that learning e-bulletins are up to date, attractive, readable and engaging. A learning e-bulletin might include the following:

- guidance on using particular services or resources
- learning tips
- information about courses and workshops
- checklists
- book reviews
- reports from staff who have attended courses, conferences or workshops
- links to additional resources
- links to multimedia resources.

E-learning

There are many different approaches to e-learning, and they include:

- web-based training packages
- use of facilitated learning communities
- use of social networking tools, e.g. blogs, Twitter.

These are described elsewhere in this book, in Chapters 4 and 7.

Electronic mailing lists

An electronic mailing list provides widespread distribution via e-mail. There are a number of different types of mailing list, including announcement lists, which carry job announcements (see www.jobs.ac.uk), and discussion lists. The latter are normally subject oriented and enable discussions to take place between subscribers to the list. A variety of organizations provide mailing lists, e.g. Google Groups provides a mailing list service; JISC Mail has a service aimed at academic communities. It is relatively simple to join (subscribe to) or leave (unsubscribe from) electronic mailing lists. In addition, it is possible to access the list's archives via its home page. Some examples include:

- MEDLIB-L@LIST.UVM.EDU – aimed at medical and health science librarians
- DIVERSITY@JISCMAIL.AC.UK – aimed at individuals interested and concerned with diversity issues
- PRISONS@JISCMAIL.AC.UK – aimed at individuals who wish to share information and good practice between prisons and public libraries in order to better support (ex-)prisoners and their families
- DELIBERATIONS-FORUM@JISCMAIL.AC.UK – an interactive, electronic web-based resource on teaching and learning in higher education
- ENDNOTE@JISCMAIL.AC.UK – shares knowledge and expertise on EndNote
- LIS-TRAINERS@JISCMAIL.AC.UK – the South West Library Information Skills Trainers Forum, which shares best practice and new approaches to training.

E-mails

E-mail offers an everyday and convenient approach to learning in the workplace. It provides:

- access to information and advice
- exchange of information and files, e.g. reading materials or reports
- access to communications on professional discussion groups
- access to professional colleagues from around the world.

However, there can be a problem of information overload, and inboxes quite often fill up with:

- useful e-mails, e.g. from colleagues and employer
- private e-mails from friends and family
- notification of news and updates from electronic mailing lists (see Electronic mailing lists) and social networking sites, e.g. LinkedIn and Facebook
- spam, i.e. unsolicited commercial e-mail.

It is therefore important to be well organized and to use e-mail tools to manage the flow and storage of e-mail messages.

E-portfolio

An e-portfolio is an electronic tool which provides access to an online space which individuals can use to build their personal development portfolio (see later in this chapter). The benefit of using an e-portfolio over a paper-based one is that it enables a person to organize, display and manage work in a wide range of formats, e.g. MS Word or PDF files, PowerPoint presentations, audio or video files, graphics and other multimedia. It is relatively easy to publish, archive or share an e-portfolio.

A popular example of a tool for creating an e-portfolio is PebblePad (see www.pebblepad.co.uk). An alternative approach to creating an e-portfolio is via a blog (see earlier in this chapter, and also Chapter 4).

Example 8.5 'Punch up your portfolio', by Katie Dunneback

In her article 'Punch up your portfolio' Katie Dunneback outlines the relevance of portfolios for librarians, and she provides a useful list of what to include:

- *Copies or links to articles you've written on topics in the field*
- *Handouts you've created for classes you've taught/developed*
- *Subject-oriented bibliographies and pathfinders*
- *Read-a-like lists*
- *Photographs of displays you've created*
- *Policies you helped to develop*
- *Craft plans and examples*
- *Grant proposals*
- *Catalogue records*
- *Copies or links to articles about you, or a listing of where to find these articles*
- *PowerPoint presentations you've given*
- *Photographs of events you've organized with quotes from participants*
- *Synopsis of book and discussion questions for a book club*
- *Links to websites you maintain*
- *Photographs of how you processed a book for preservation*
- *Circulation statistics of collections you manage*
- *Collection development plans*
- *Flyers for programmes you put on*
- *Links to databases you developed*
- *Summary of your thesis research*
- *Link to a streaming audio archive of a presentation that you gave.*

This is an impressive list and it gives an idea of the range of items that can be included in an e-portfolio. The content of an e-portfolio needs to be linked together through items such as a personal statement and curriculum vitae. See Personal development planning and Personal development portfolios later in this chapter.

Evaluating different products

A constant stream of new products, services and resources is available for use by library and information workers. Evaluating different products is a source of learning in the workplace, as it provides an opportunity to:

- update knowledge and skills
- develop critical thinking skills
- develop communication skills, e.g. producing a summary report, poster or presentation on your findings.

Case study 8.12 Evaluating a learning innovation

Jane was asked to evaluate a number of different learning innovations for possible inclusion in a training event for students. She used the following guidelines to evaluate four different games:

- Will the innovation enable us to achieve the intended learning outcome(s)?
- Is the innovation appropriate to the student audience?
  - Are there any diversity issues?
  - Are there any disability issues?
- Practical aspects:
  - What is involved?
  - What will it cost?
  - How long will the activity take?

Jane created a table using these evaluation criteria, and this helped the trainers to select the required game.

Exchanges

An exchange is a useful means of staff development. It involves two members of staff swapping roles for a period of time. The exchange can take place between staff in different libraries within the same library service, region or country, or in different countries. The period of exchange may be as short as a week or as long as a year.

Exchanges offer a unique approach to individual workplace learning and the library gains from having a new member of staff who is likely to bring a different skill-set and perspectives. The American Library Association supports librarians by offering international opportunities and funding sources (see www.ala.org), as does the UK's Chartered Institute of Library and Information Professionals (CILIP) through its LIBEX international job exchange programme. The detailed reports from librarians who have completed an exchange provide an insight to their experiences (see www.cilip.org.uk).

Example 8.6 Exchanging Canada for Australia

Katharine Ball (2010) writes an interesting report on her exchange experience and she concludes: 'A work exchange is an interesting experience that I would recommend to anyone – both for professional and personal growth.'

Exhibitions

Many library and information conferences hold exhibitions, e.g. of publishers or database suppliers, and they can be a useful source of up-to-date information and ideas. As well as freebies! To get the most out of attending exhibitions, it is worthwhile:

* preparing for them by identifying your desired outcomes
* producing a report, blog entry or poster presentation as a means of disseminating findings to colleagues.

Exit interviews

An exit interview takes place just before an employee leaves the library or information service. It provides a unique opportunity to:

* gain insights into what works well or could be improved
* gain off-the-record information
* gain general feedback
* thank the leaving member of staff for their contributions.

A useful approach to getting the best out of an exit interview is to arrange it in advance and send a list of questions so that the person concerned has time to reflect on them. Typical questions could include:

* What has been the best thing about working in this library? And what has been the worst?
* What could we do better?
* What could we do differently?
* What should we stop doing?
* What advice would you give to the person taking on your role?

External funding

Obtaining external funding for a project is one way of introducing learning into the workplace. Projects may be funded by international bodies, government agencies, specialist bodies or voluntary organizations. Projects may be delivered by a single library or by a group of libraries either within the same region or country or an international group. Working towards achieving external funding, gaining the funding and then implementing the project provides opportunities for learning about:

- bidding processes
- project plans and budgets
- managing and implementing a project, including the use of software tools such as Microsoft Project
- working in a project team and/or in a collaborative and diverse team
- communicating and reporting on the project
- disseminating news on the project's progress and outcomes, e.g. via a website, blog or conferences.

Feedback

This is an extremely important approach to learning in the workplace. Giving and receiving constructive feedback helps to create a learning culture and enables librarians to learn from each other. Effective feedback is:

- designed to improve performance
- delivered in a timely manner (as soon as possible after the event)
- sensitively structured and presented
- descriptive rather than evaluative.

Standard practice in giving feedback is to:

- start with a positive
- make a suggestion for change or improvement
- end on a positive.

Case study 8.13 Giving feedback

Janet, an information service director, spent some time thinking about how to give feedback to a new recruit, Mike, who was a sensitive and shy young man. She used the structure given above and the following form of words:

- I am pleased with the way in which you have settled into work and started to establish positive relationships with your colleagues.
- I've noticed that you sometimes leave a customer in the middle of a query and go to answer the phone. This should have been covered in your induction training and I know there is always a lot to remember at the start of a new job. For us, it is important that we always complete one query before responding to another customer. If you can

remember this in future, then it will make working on the help desk less stressful – someone in the back office will always pick up the phone after five rings.
• Overall, you are doing a good job. Both information service staff and customers are saying positive things about you. Well done.

Fishbone diagram

A fishbone diagram (also called an Ishikawa diagram) is useful for identifying possible causes of a problem. It can be completed as a group activity, and so enhances group understanding of a particular problem. The procedure for drawing a fishbone diagram is relatively simple:

1 Write the name of the problem on the right-hand side of a piece of paper and draw a box around it.
2 Draw a horizontal line running across the paper to the box (this is the backbone of the fish).
3 Brainstorm about the causes of the problem. Sometimes general themes can be used to identify the causes, e.g. environment, people, finance, suppliers, methods, management. Write these general categories as branches of the backbone.
4 For each theme identify potential causes and write these down on smaller lines branching off from the general categories. Sometimes a potential cause will occur under a number of different categories.
5 For each of these causes ask the reason why and produce a sub-cause. Continue this process until you have run out of ideas.
6 As a group, reflect on what you have learnt about the problem. Consider the gaps in the fishbone diagram. Have you missed something out?

Figure 8.1 illustrates a fishbone diagram. A fishbone diagram template can be obtained from the internet.[2]

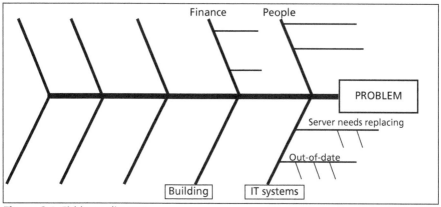

Figure 8.1 *Fishbone diagram*

Focus groups

The concept of a focus group comes from the world of marketing, where it is used to find out the views of a group of customers or potential customers. Nowadays, it is widely used in organizations as a means of obtaining feedback from service users and from employees. Establishing a focus group linked to a particular theme or initiative is often a productive approach to identifying user needs. Bloor et al. (2001) provide detailed guidance on the use of focus groups.

Establishing a focus group normally involves:

- identifying the aim of the focus group
- working out practical arrangements – who will facilitate it, how it will be structured (normally there is a very loose structure), who will be invited, where/when will it be held, how feedback will be recorded
- obtaining ethics clearance. If the focus group is being carried out as part of an evaluative research project, then ethics clearance is normally obtained via the organization's ethics (or equivalent) group
- identifying the focus group members to the meeting
- running the meeting
- reporting the findings
- thanking the participants.

Case study 8.14 Understanding students' discovery tool preferences

Sarah Elsegood (2012, 24) provides a very detailed case study of the use of a focus group to help understand students' discovery tool preferences. She writes:

> How do students look for information and do our search tools meet students' needs? We set up a focus group to discover how our users actually find information and which resources they choose to use. Answering these questions is helpful when making decisions relating to the configuration of our search tools.

It is interesting to note that focus groups are often a two-way learning process, and one of the students commented 'Everyone in the whole university should do this group, then everybody would know all this stuff that we didn't know before we came in this room'. (Elsegood, 2012, 28).

Frequently asked questions

Library and information services receive the same or similar questions time and time again. These frequently asked questions (FAQs) are an important learning resource for staff. They can be made available via a website, VLE, portal, blog, e-mail or in print. The processes both of collecting and presenting FAQs and of using them on a day-to-day basis provide opportunities for learning. The list will need to be updated at regular intervals.

Case study 8.15 FAQs and student helpers

In a business school a group of student helpers were recruited to help train new undergraduates in referencing techniques. They received special training to ensure that they provided correct advice. The library staff had prepared a list of the FAQs which they received at the information help desk. The list of FAQs was used as an informal assessment exercise, carried out in pairs, at the end of the training workshop for the student helpers. At the end of the six-week peer-learning scheme, the student helpers were brought together for a debriefing and evaluation workshop. One of the activities in this workshop was to add to the list of FAQs, based on their own experiences. This list would then be used in the following year's student helpers' scheme.

Gap year

At one time, a gap year was the province of young people who travelled the world and/or volunteered for a year before or after completing their first degree and before entering their chosen career. More recently, an increasing number of people are taking gap years either mid-career or towards the end of their career.

Advantages:

- It provides an opportunity for developing new knowledge and skills.
- It may remotivate someone and recharge their career aspirations.
- It provides an opportunity for bringing in a temporary worker with new and different ideas.

Disadvantages:

- It is often extremely expensive for the person going on the gap year, who won't receive a salary.
- It is outside of the range of possibilities for many people.
- It is likely to involve library managers in extensive work to have a replacement person recruited and inducted.
- The person on the gap year may be disillusioned with their previous position when they return.
- The person on the gap year may take some time to settle back into their original role.

Case study 8.16 A trip around the world

Amanda obtained 12 months' unpaid leave from her position in a university and sailed around the world on a tall ship. Working and living in confined quarters with a small group of people helped her to develop her interpersonal skills. She also gained a husband! On returning to work, she had renewed enthusiasm and motivation for her job and decided to complete a master's programme as a way of developing her career.

Induction

Induction of new staff or of staff promoted to a new position provides a learning opportunity for both the person being inducted and also the people delivering the induction. The induction process is likely to take place over a series of weeks, and even months, and may involve a range of activities, including:

- tour of library and of other buildings
- introduction to colleagues and wider team
- introduction to mentor or buddy
- meetings, e.g. with manager(s) and other key stakeholders
- training events
- online tutorials
- one-to-one briefings and coaching sessions
- induction review meetings, e.g. with trainer or manager.

Many library and information services have very well structured induction processes and the participants are asked to maintain an induction portfolio in which they record their learning. This portfolio forms the basis of induction review meetings.

Instructions

The process of giving instructions provides an opportunity for learning. Before you give instructions to another person or group, there are a few rules to observe:

- Keep the instructions as simple as possible.
- Make sure that they are logical.
- Pilot them before use.

When you are giving instructions it is worthwhile to:

- make sure that the other person is listening
- use an appropriate tone, e.g. 'ask' rather than 'tell'
- use simple words and short sentences
- start with the reason for the instructions – what the purpose is
- indicate the number of steps
- check for understanding (at the end of each step and also at the end of the process)
- make the ending clear
- provide a written summary.

Example 8.7 The wrong instructions!

The author attended a one-day workshop. Towards the end of a long morning session, the facilitator said 'We will now have coffee, but before we have a break there is one more exercise to do ...'. After the first five words most people, including the author, had left or were leaving the room. This left a 'messy' situation for the facilitator to sort out. If he had said 'We have one more exercise to do and then we will have a coffee break', there would have been no problem of people responding in different ways.

Internet

There are numerous opportunities for learning and development via the internet. These can be individual or group activities. An indicative list of learning opportunities includes:

* apps
* blogs
* e-learning
* e-mail
* online conferences
* online discussion groups
* publisher and supplier websites
* web-based training courses
* websites from other libraries and information services.

Further information and ideas are available in Chapter 4.

Interviews

Interviews offer an opportunity for learning in different situations:

* Selection interviews offer an opportunity for learning for both the candidate and the members of the panel.
* Research interviews offer an opportunity for the interviewer to learn from the person being interviewed, who will, hopefully, learn from reflecting on their practice.
* Organizational review interviews occur when someone is interviewed about their particular role and contribution to the library and information service, offering learning opportunities to both parties.

Learning from interviewing involves:

* Before the interview
    — The interviewer will prepare the interview and be clear as to its aim, objectives, structure and questions. S/he also needs to organize the

venue and plan how the interview will be recorded, e.g. notes, audio recording.
— In the case of selection interviews, the person being interviewed will prepare by learning about the sector, organization, department, and will prepare for anticipated questions.
— In the case of other interviews, the person being interviewed may not be involved in preparatory activities.
• During the interview
— First, there will be introductions, explanation about the purpose and structure of the interview.
— The interviewer will ask a series of structured questions and record the answers.
— There is likely to be time for the person being interviewed to add their own comments.
— Finally, the interviewer will thank the interviewee and explain what happens next.
• After the interview
— The interviewer reports the outcomes of the interview and completes any documentation/reports.
— The interviewer contacts the interviewee and thanks them for their contribution.

Job rotation

This is a technique which enables individuals to rotate either their whole job or part of their job with others, in a structured manner. It has a number of benefits:

• Individuals learn how to carry out a number of tasks and activities within the library.
• Long-term employees may find that it helps to remotivate them and so helps to reduce professional stagnation.
• It leads to multi-skilling.
• It creates additional back-up, e.g. for holidays or during periods of high demand.

One of the disadvantages of job rotation is that it may reduce productivity as individuals learn how to carry out a new task. It is possible that some positions and activities may not be suitable for job rotation, e.g. dealing with people issues. There may be contractual issues which prevent job rotation, and some people may have a negative approach to it.

Case study 8.17 Job rotation at the Niger Delta University Library

Baro (2012) describes a job rotation programme which was first introduced in 1994. His article indicates that the job rotation programme had the following benefits:

- acquisition of new skills by librarians
- greater productivity and job satisfaction
- development of new relationships across the university library
- development of new skills for career enhancement.

Key performance indicators

A KPI is a measure used to evaluate the success (or otherwise) of a particular activity. Typically, KPIs are aligned to help the library and information service meet its strategic aims which, in turn, will be aligned to the strategic aims of the parent organization. There are different kinds of KPI, such as:

- directional indicator which indicates whether or not something is improving
- quantitative indicator
- financial indicator.

Example 8.8 Library and Information Health Network North West

This group (see www.lihnn.nhs.uk) provides examples of KPIs for health libraries. The list includes examples such as:

- 50% of the Trust staff will be registered with the library.
- 30 members of Trust staff will attend Information Skills Training each month.
- 100% of literature searches will be completed in 2 days or less.

The process of identifying and then working towards and achieving a KPI provides opportunities for individuals and teams to learn and develop.

Learning boxes

The concept of a learning box comes from the work of Peter Honey (1994) and is one approach to making learning visible in the workplace. Learning boxes can be physically placed in key positions in the library, or an online version can be provided on an intranet or portal, e.g. using a discussion board tool. Individual members of staff post entries with the following structure:

- brief description of a particular situation
- what was learnt or relearnt from the experience
- what will be done better or differently as a result of this learning experience.

At regular intervals, e.g. monthly, the entries are sorted into categories such as:

- everyday or routine experiences
- unusual, novel and one-off experiences
- mistakes
- successes.

These are then displayed and/or discussed at a meeting. This approach to learning, which is a public approach to learning-journal entries, helps to establish a learning culture and share individuals' learning experiences.

Learning contracts

A learning contract is a formal agreement between at least two people, specifying a learning process. A learning contract may include the following information:

- learning aim
- learning outcome(s)
- proposed learning activity or activities
- method of assessing or reviewing learning
- resource requirements
- support requirements
- milestones and target date(s).

Learning contracts can be used as part of an appraisal or performance process, or they can be used as a separate activity.

Example 8.9 Example learning contract
Figure 8.2 presents an example of a learning contract. It illustrates the structure and headings used, and also how it should be completed.

Learning conversations

Learning conversations are an important approach to introducing learning as an integral part of daily life in a library and information service. Learning conversations involve introducing learning and reflection on learning into conversations between individuals or within the context of meetings. They involve asking questions such as:

- What can we learn from this?
- How can we improve this?
- How do we prevent this from happening in future?

The real value of learning conversations is that they integrate learning into everyday life, and this means that difficult situations can be transformed into learning opportunities. Introducing the phrase 'learning conversation' into the

Name of staff member	Thomas Mason
Name of team leader	Jane Smith
Learning aim	To develop skills in dealing with challenging customers
Learning outcome(s)	1 To be able to use a number of standard procedures when dealing with customers 2 To be able to manage challenging customers in a calm and relaxed manner
Proposed learning activity or activities	1 To attend the in-house workshop on 'dealing with challenging customers' 2 To attend a workshop on 'managing stress' 3 To shadow Jean (an experienced member of staff) when she is working on the Help Desk, for at least 3 hours 4 To keep a diary and reflect on his experience of working on the Help Desk
Method of assessing or reviewing learning	Thomas to report progress to Jane after a 4- and 8-week period. If necessary, Jane to observe Thomas working at the Help Desk
Resource requirements	Cost of attending two workshops. Time involved in attending workshops
Support requirements	Jane to provide Thomas with support
Milestones and target date(s)	Completion of both workshops Completion of shadowing activity Review meetings at 4 and 8 weeks
Signatures and date	

Figure 8.2 *Example learning contract*

workplace helps to highlight and underline that learning is taking place.

Learning journals

A learning journal is a simple tool for recording, structuring and reflecting on learning experiences. As with a diary, individuals can maintain a regular journal. A particular incident or critical experience may form the focus of an entry or series of entries. A learning journal can be maintained in different ways:

- in a notebook
- by sending yourself e-mails
- in a blog (see Chapter 4).

A simple approach to structuring a learning-journal entry involves completing the following:

- outline of the event (in fewer than 50 words)
- identification of what you learnt as a result of reflecting on the event

- identification of what you will do differently next time.

Meetings

Meetings provide an important opportunity for learning in the workplace. Different learning activities can be scheduled into meetings, including:

- analysing mistakes
- asking for advice
- use of audio recordings, e.g. to listen to a short speech or input, or to record a section of a meeting and reflect on it
- brainstorming
- celebrating success
- delegation
- review of KPIs
- learning conversations
- demonstrations
- displays
- management tools such as a SWOT analysis, metaphors and stories
- mind mapping
- multimedia resources, e.g. videos
- Post-it® notes
- praise and rewards
- self-assessment questionnaires
- setting deadlines
- sticky notes
- surveys
- teamwork.

These examples are all described elsewhere in this chapter.

Example 8.10 Improving the quality of meetings

A relatively new team leader, Jouharah, asked a colleague to sit in on one of her team meetings and give feedback on her performance. This took place and she learnt from the feedback that she was well organized and managed the meeting well. One learning point was that she needed to think about how to include quieter members of the team in the discussions.

Mentoring

Mentoring is a process that involves learning from a more experienced practitioner, and it is often used to promote development and progression in the workplace (Cox, Bachkirova and Clutterbuck, 2009). Career structures have changed in the past thirty years, from a traditional, hierarchical, stable structure to one that takes a variety of forms and requires individuals to take charge of their own destiny and manage their career process (Briscoe and Hall, 2006). Originally, mentoring was viewed as a relationship between an early-career or 'young' person and a more experienced or 'wise' person, but this traditional model has been replaced by the idea of a mentoring relationship which is more equitable, perhaps short-term or loosely connected. In addition, the mentee may want to learn specific skills or gain particular opportunities from the mentor, rather than become more like their mentor.

Some library and information services provide formal mentoring schemes, e.g. for new recruits, or for staff who may find barriers to their career progression. Informal mentoring often takes place when an individual identifies a colleague (either within their own organization or in another one). This is illustrated in the following case study.

Case study 8.18 Mentoring

Jane wanted to develop her career as a law librarian and had obtained her first position in a law firm in London. Her new colleagues had all worked with the firm for at least ten years and she was unsure that her new team leader would be able to help her with careers advice. At a law librarians' event Jane met a very experienced law librarian, Lindsay, who had worked in a number of different firms for the last 12 years and they got on well together. Jane decided to ask Lindsay to be her mentor. Lindsay readily agreed and they agreed that they would work together by having monthly or six-weekly early-evening meetings in a coffee bar near to their offices. They met up in this way for almost two years and during this time Jane appreciated the help and advice that she received from Lindsay. Lindsay also gained from the mentoring process and said it gave her an opportunity 'to give back' to an early-career colleague and also helped her to reflect on her own knowledge and skills. The relationship changed when Jane achieved a promotion to a more senior position in another library and Lindsay went to live in Australia. They decided that they would maintain e-mail contact and corresponded with each other at irregular intervals.

Example 8.11 Mentoring as part of gaining a professional qualification

CILIP provides guidance and support through mentoring for individuals working towards their professional qualifications. The materials available include the Mentor Scheme Guidelines (including mentoring agreement template), Chartership Handbook and the Professional Knowledge and Skills Base. CILIP also offers training and support for mentors and for individuals working towards their professional qualification. Useful sources of information include:

www.cilip.org.uk
www.careerdevelopmentgroup.org.uk

Metaphors

A metaphor is an analogy, anecdote or story that puts across a message. They are a useful means of delivering a complex or even unwelcome message. Most people enjoy stories and they will listen to them and take their own meaning from them. Metaphors can be delivered in a conversational manner at work, e.g. in meetings, over lunch, at the photocopier.

Case study 8.19 A major reorganization (originally published in Allan, 1999)

A university library was moving from five buildings into four buildings. The whole service was being reorganized and resources from each building were being moved to different locations. The co-ordinating group built up a complex picture of what moves had to take place and in which order. Unless everyone understood the process, there was considerable scope for chaos.

One staff member developed the metaphor of an airport with internal and external flights, and different arrival and departure lounges. This metaphor was used to explain to all staff the complex change process. The metaphor was further developed to include fog, emergency breakdowns and lost luggage. This helped to prepare all staff for the need to be flexible and to respond to unexpected situations.

Mind mapping

Mind mapping (see also Chapter 4) was developed by Tony Buzan (1989) and it provides a quick and easy approach to helping someone to:

- organize ideas
- generate ideas
- develop a memory aid
- summarize ideas
- develop a structure, e.g. for a presentation or project.

Mind maps apparently work as they stimulate both the left- and right-hand sides of the brain. The mapping process involves:

- placing a central idea or theme in the centre of a piece of paper. Decorate it with colour, images or symbols.
- drawing a number of main branches from this idea. Along each main branch write the name of a key idea. Decorate each branch with colour, images or symbols.
- drawing smaller branches from each of the main branches. Decorate with colour, images or symbols.
- adding even smaller branches to these branches. Decorate with colour, images or symbols.

- leaving some gaps (this will help to stimulate ideas).

Mind maps can be produced simply, on paper, or through online tools such as www.thinkbuzan.com, freemind.sourceforge.net, or www.mindgenius.com.

Networking

Networking is concerned with developing connections with colleagues as a means of helping and supporting each other. The starting-point for networking is meeting and getting to know like-minded people and a good starting-point is people with whom there is a shared experience, e.g. fellow students from a library or information course, current or past colleagues. An important part of conferences is that they provide an opportunity for networking. Online networking via tools such as LinkedIn is now extremely popular (see Chapter 4).

What are the benefits of networking? It can provide:

- access to information and ideas
- access to news about forthcoming vacancies
- help and support with project bids
- general support and guidance.

What are the challenges of networking?

- Not everyone finds it easy to do.
- It does take up time.
- It is important to focus on becoming part of networks that are relevant to your interests and ambitions.

Tips on networking are:

- Remember that networking is based on the concept of 'give and take'.
- Be interested in others and willing to provide them with support and help.
- Keep your promises.

Newsletters

See E-bulletins.

Online discussion groups

Online discussion groups provide a convenient method for groups to communicate with each other using the internet. Message or bulletin boards enable people to post messages which are then read and responded to by others. This is sometimes called asynchronous communications, as the people involved in the discussions are not logged into the system at the same time but post their messages when it is convenient for them to do so. Access to online discussions may be through electronic mailing lists (see earlier in this chapter), discussion boards available through professional body websites such as ALA and CILIP, or discussion boards in VLEs.

Online tutorials

Online tutorials are often available to support users of computer software and products, and other resources. They have a number of advantages for learners, who can:

- learn at their own pace
- repeat sections if unclear
- fit them around other work
- print off key points.

Disadvantages include:

- Some people don't like this approach to learning.
- They don't offer a very personalized approach to learning.
- They can be time consuming.

Many suppliers of commonly used software or databases provide online tutorials as in the following examples:

- www.endnote.com/training
- www.ieee.org/publications_standards
- www.nlm.nih.gov/bsdd/disted/pubmedtutorial/
- www.refworks.com/tutorial
- www.support.epnet.com/training/.

In addition, many libraries and information services provide their own online tutorials for their customers and/or staff. Examples include:

- http://library/leeds.ac.uk/skills-online-tutorials
- www.thecochranelibrary.com
- www.lib.ncsu.edu/tutorials
- www.eel.nhs.uk/Home/Training/Elearningtutorials.aspx.

Organizing events

There is an extremely wide range of events that may be held in library and information services, including:

- careers events
- conferences
- family history days
- induction or training events
- visits, workshops and readings by a poet-in-residence
- professional meetings
- visits by authors or poets
- visits, workshops and readings by a writer-in-residence.

Organizing an event can help individual library and information workers to develop a range of skills, including:

- communication
- entrepreneurial
- financial – including fund raising
- marketing and PR
- networking
- presentation
- project management
- teamworking.

Personal development planning

Personal development planning (PDP) is a process which helps individuals to think about their learning, performance and achievements and to plan for their continuing career development. The basis of PDP is some fundamental learning processes involving:

- identification of career or development goal
- identification of current practice or achievements, e.g. through a curriculum vitae, personal statement, or feedback from appraisal or performance reviews
- reflection on current practice or achievements
- production of an action plan
- implementation of the action plan
- evaluation of progress.

PDP may be carried out for a number of reasons, such as:

- part of library and information services talent development processes
- working towards a professional qualification
- providing a focus for working with a mentor
- personal satisfaction and desire to progress one's career.

Personal development portfolios

A personal development portfolio is a tool which enables individuals to become involved in and to evidence personal development planning (see previous section) in a structured manner by:

- assessing their knowledge, skills and experience
- reflecting on their learning and performance
- establishing personal, educational, employment and career goals.

Typically, a personal development portfolio provides access to a range of materials, including:

- curriculum vitae
- personal statement(s)
- assessment of strengths and weaknesses, e.g. against a competency framework
- development plan(s)
- supporting statements, e.g. from managers, colleagues, customers
- records of learning activities, e.g. training attended, qualifications.

These materials can be organized in a paper-based file or in an electronic file or portfolio. Personal development portfolios are used in a number of different ways, including:

- when applying for a new position
- when applying for a professional qualification
- to help boost self-esteem.

Example 8.12 Becoming a chartered librarian

The route to obtaining chartered status in the UK involves developing a personal development portfolio. The CILIP website (www.cilip.org.uk/jobs-careers) provides detailed advice and guidance on developing a personal portfolio, including information on portfolio-building courses.

Example 8.13 Online portfolios

A personal development portfolio can be kept as a private document or shared through a blog or electronic portfolio, e.g. a library student on the MLIS course at University College, Dublin, maintained an e-portfolio via his blog.[3] Another blog which provides advice and insights into personal development portfolios is Laura's Dark Archive.[4]

Playing cards

The use of games in training and development is outlined in Chapter 3. The following case study describes the use of 'fire cards' in helping to put across a health and safety message in an engaging manner.

Case study 8.20 Fire exits

A library training officer, Mark, had the challenge of working with the health and safety officer to ensure that all library staff knew where the fire exits were in each building, and the evacuation procedures. One of the difficulties was that the library was spread over six different buildings and staff frequently covered for each other. Staff attended formal briefings in their work teams. In addition, Mark developed a set of red 'fire cards' and each staff member was given a card. They were then asked to give each other one of these cards at different times of the working day. The card stated 'The fire alarm has gone off. What do you do now?' On receiving a card, the recipient had to answer the question. This game generated a lot of interest in the fire procedures and exit routes, and resulted in staff developing their knowledge of fire safety procedures. Overall, Mark thought the use of these cards was a useful strategy for creating an interest in, enthusiasm for and knowledge of fire procedures.

Post-it® notes

See Sticky notes.

Presentations

Developing effective presentation skills is important for library and information workers, who may be asked to give presentations to their customers or other staff. Supervisors and managers are often required to make presentations, and they are also often part of recruitment processes for senior staff. Chapter 3 provides advice and guidance on presentations.

In terms of helping library and information workers to develop their presentation skills, there are a range of opportunities, including:

- mini-presentations in meetings
- involvement in staff training events
- involvement in induction and orientation events
- talks to customers, visitors or suppliers.

For some people, working with a colleague helps to make it easier to present, while other people prefer to be in sole control of the presentation.

Case study 8.21 Enhancing presentation skills

A university library worker, Suzanna, was terrified of making presentations, and although she attended a one-day training course it didn't give her the confidence she needed to stand up in front of groups. From a friend, she learnt about possibilities for selling children's books from home and signed up as a sales consultant. This new role forced her to make presentations at regular intervals, and after a few months she had gained in confidence. She then began volunteering to make presentations at work.

Professional journals

Professional journals provide news, articles, book reviews, advice columns, advertisements and job vacancies for a professional group, e.g. librarians in general, or for a specific group of librarians, such as law or music librarians. They are an important means of keeping up to date and of learning about current practice and issues in the profession. Some examples include:

- *American Libraries* magazine (see www.americanlibraries.org)
- *Australian Library Journal* (see www.alia.org.au)
- *CILIP Update* (see www.cilip.org.uk)
- *Teacher Librarian* (see www.teacherlibrarian.com)
- *The Researching Librarian* (see www.researchinglibrarian.com).

Professional organizations

There are many different professional organizations in the world of library and information work, including:

- international associations
- national associations and their special groups
- organizations concerned with a particular geographical region
- specialist groups, e.g. aimed at a particular type of librarianship, such as law or health services.

In addition to specialist library and information organizations, there are others that are very relevant to learning in the workplace, and these include associations covering topics such as project management, specific VLEs, e-learning and training practice.

Professional organizations offer a wide range of services which may include many of the following:

- development of policy and practices
- canvassing and lobbying on key issues
- careers help and guidance
- continuing professional development
- professional journals (see previous section) and bulletins
- networking opportunities
- special membership services

- library and information services.

Each has its own goal and is aimed at a particular group of library and information workers. There are normally different levels of membership, e.g. student, associate, full member, fellow, retired member, as well as institutional member. Joining one or more professional associations is an important method of keeping up to date and engaging with professional communities of interest and communities of practice.

Project work

Projects provide a useful means of enabling learning in the workplace. Many libraries have a range of projects that require management, and examples include:

- design of induction events for staff or customers
- signage and guiding projects
- social media projects
- design and implementation of new systems or procedures
- library moves or refurbishment projects
- initiatives funded by external bodies.

Projects provide a useful means for staff to gain experience and skills in areas such as:

- project management
- time management
- staff management
- teamwork
- working with people from different departments or organizations
- managing finances
- communication and presentation
- report writing
- monitoring and controlling.

Case study 8.22 Introducing social media into an independent library

Shona worked in a library in a major building and contracting company. She wanted to develop the use of social media but was not sure how to establish and manage the overall project. Consequently, she attended a one-day workshop on project management that was aimed at librarians and also read a short guide to the subject. She looked at the JISC website (www.jisc.ac.uk), which provided very detailed guidance on running a JISC project. Although this guidance was too detailed for her purposes, it gave her a helpful checklist of project management tools and techniques. She had access to MS Project at work and taught herself to use it. With the support of these project management tools and techniques, Shona managed to introduce a library blog. This experience gave her confidence to apply for a different library role, and one which involved managing a number of projects.

Promotion

Applying for or gaining promotion provides many learning opportunities. This is illustrated in the following case studies.

Case study 8.23 Applying for promotion

Xue Mei applied for promotion within her company in order to move from assistant librarian to resources librarian. She put a lot of time and effort into her application and was very disappointed not to be promoted. She asked for a feedback interview and learnt that although her interview went well, she did not have sufficient experience in supervising staff. She arranged with her manager that she would supervise two new office apprentices and attend a training workshop on Supervising Staff.

Case study 8.24 Gaining promotion

Mark was promoted to a Research Officer position within a government library and information service. He was thrilled to receive the promotion and thought that he was 'a perfect fit' for the new role. However, by the end of the first month he was struggling. In discussions with his line manager he realized that his communication style was jarring with some of his quite senior new customers and that he needed to develop a much more professional approach to his role. Working with his line manager, he identified and put into practice an action plan. Two months later he had made the necessary changes, which meant that he was working and communicating very effectively with his new customers and colleagues.

QR codes

A QR or quick response code is a computer-generated code which can be used to disseminate information. They are described in Chapter 4.

Quality assurance activities

Quality assurance is concerned with using systematic processes and measures (i.e. it is a process-centred approach) to help to assure the quality of a product or service. The basis of quality assurance is a reiterative cycle (plan, do, check, act). Examples of quality assurance tools include the ISO 9000 standard (see www.iso.org); the NHS Library Quality Assurance Framework;[5] and the Public Library Quality Improvement Matrix (Scottish Library and Information Council).[6]

Quality assurance processes provide a systematic approach to measuring and using evidence-based methods for improving a service or product. Consequently, they provide opportunities for learning and development for individuals, teams and the whole service.

Quizzes

Quizzes provide a means of enabling people to learn by:

- demonstrating what they know or don't know about a particular topic (diagnostic quizzes)
- providing a tool for reflection (management development and learning style tools)
- providing opportunities for team building (quizzes used within the context of a game or structured team-development event)
- providing opportunities for fun or to raise energy levels so as to create a learning environment.

In addition, the process of developing, piloting and running a quiz also provides a learning opportunity. The use of quizzes as a learning and teaching method is described in Chapter 3, and the use of technology to help create quizzes is described in Chapter 4.

Reading

An obvious and sometimes under-used approach to learning in the workplace is through reading, e.g. e-bulletins, blogs and professional journals. Colleagues can be encouraged to read by:

- establishing a training and development blog
- circulating key items and asking for comments
- placing printouts of key items on a staff notice board
- circulating news, brief articles or reports by e-mail
- establishing a book or reading club.

Reflection

Reflection provides an important source of learning and insight into current library and information practices. According to the *Chambers Twentieth Century Dictionary*, the word 'reflect' means to bend or turn back or turn aside, to be mirrored or to meditate. Although a relatively simple process, reflection does involve:

- making time for the activity
- structuring reflection, e.g. by asking questions
- developing an action plan.

The types of questions which support reflective practice include:

- What has happened?

- What worked well?
- What could be improved?
- What have I learnt from this situation?
- What will I do differently next time?

Learning journals are a structured approach to reflection. They are described earlier in this chapter.

Retreats or residentials

A retreat or residential experience provides welcome opportunities to reflect and learn away from the everyday stresses and pressures of the workplace. The advantages of this approach to learning and development are:

- They are intensive experiences.
- The focus may be on a workplace issue or problem.
- They provide an opportunity for bringing people together, perhaps from different departments in a large company.
- They provide an opportunity for team building and networking.
- They enable individuals and teams to reflect on their experiences.

The disadvantages of this approach include:

- They require individuals to be away from the workplace.
- They are relatively expensive, e.g. there are travel and accommodation costs.
- They need to be carefully facilitated (which is also an additional cost).

Example 8.14 Change Academy

The author is involved in leading a Change Academy process (see www.heacademy.ac.uk) which brings together a team from across a university, representing library and information services, student services, disability services and academic schools. The purpose is to develop and introduce a whole-university process for the development of information skills. The process began with a residential retreat which enabled the team to:

- form and develop working relationships
- identify and develop a strategy
- develop an action plan.

Following the retreat, the project team is working and meeting regularly. It has a nine-months' schedule of work to complete.

Rich pictures

The concept of a 'rich picture' comes from soft systems methodology and it provides a method of articulating and capturing individuals' understanding about a complex problem or issue. Rich pictures can be quickly produced and involve identifying the people and systems involved in a particular situation, and the connections between them. There are very few rules about producing rich pictures, except that they are likely to include:

- pictures, e.g. of people, buildings, systems
- arrows which show the interconnections between the pictures.

No artistic skills are required, e.g. people can be represented in a 'matchstick' format. A search on Google for 'rich pictures' throws up many different examples which could be used to brief a team before they produce their own rich picture.

Secondment

A secondment is a temporary posting in another position, which may be within the same organization or in a different one. A secondment provides an individual with an opportunity to develop their knowledge, skills and experience, and also to broaden their networks. For the host library or information service, secondments provide an opportunity to fill a vacancy temporarily and to gain a new member of staff with different perspectives. Secondments provide a pathway to leadership and management positions (see Ritchie, 2007).

Case study 8.25 Secondment opportunities and issues at Queensland University of Technology Library

Uthmann (2005) provides an interesting account of secondment opportunities and issues at Queensland University of Technology Library and notes some of the challenges of organizing and working on secondment. Lessons learnt from the experience include the importance of: managing everyone's expectations; supporting the secondee in getting up to speed in their new role; managing the role in terms of short- and long-term goals and projects and being aware that long-term activities will be dependent on the length of the secondment; providing support for the secondee when they return to their substantive post.

Self-assessment tools

An extensive range of self-assessment tools are available, and these provide opportunities for self-reflection and learning. Popular examples include self-assessment tools on subjects such as:

- emotional intelligence
- leadership style
- learning styles

- organizational development
- personality
- teamwork
- time management
- training skills.

Some tools are available free on the internet, while others may be used only by trained occupational psychologists.

Case study 8.26 Time management

Nigel led a team of indexers in a government department. There were problems of time management with one team member (James). As a means of tackling the issue, Nigel asked his colleague to complete a time management quiz (available free from www.mindtools. com). The results were then discussed and James agreed to an action plan to improve his time management. Reflecting on the experience, Nigel felt that the self-assessment tool had helped the process, as it gave a structure to the discussion and prevented it from becoming too intense.

Self-paced tutorials
See Online tutorials.

Setting deadlines
The process of setting and meeting deadlines is an important workplace skill both for individuals and for leaders and managers. When setting and agreeing deadlines it is important to:

- be realistic
- be specific
- include time for contingencies
- agree how progress will be monitored and reviewed
- write them down, e.g. confirm agreement by an e-mail.

Case study 8.27 Meeting deadlines

Bushra, a team leader in a reference library, had problems caused by one of her team members (Nigel) not meeting deadlines. She discussed this as part of his appraisal and agreed the following actions:

- He would keep a separate list of deadlines and check these at least twice a week.
- He would inform her in advance if he did not think that he would be able to meet a particular deadline.
- They would review progress together on a monthly basis.

The result of this action plan was that Nigel improved his ability to meet deadlines, and when he thought he was going to miss one he always informed Bushra in advance.

Speed networking

As its name suggests this is networking (see earlier in this chapter) at speed. Typically, individuals are given three to five minutes in which to network.

Case study 8.28 Speed networking

Julie Hoskins (2012) provides a conference report on CILIP's Career Development Group conference. She writes:

> We were all called together to be sorted into two groups for our speed networking session. In our groups of 3 people we had 3 minutes to tell the others who we were, where we worked, our role and what made us unique. … The session was a brilliant use of time and some of the more organized members had business cards to swap. I know we all met a couple of people whom we will be e-mailing in the not too distant future.

Sticky notes

Sticky notes or Post-it® notes are a piece of stationery with a sticky edge. It is now possible to obtain these notes in a wide range of colours, shapes and sizes. They can be used for:

- action planning
- generating ideas
- generating questions
- giving feedback and praise
- obtaining quick feedback
- planning a presentation
- planning a project
- reminding yourself about something
- saying thank you.

Study tours

Study tours are a means by which a group of library and information workers can visit a group of different libraries. These may be located in a particular city, region or country, or have a specific theme. Study tours provide individual librarians with an opportunity to learn about a group of libraries, network with library and information workers in the host libraries and with other members of the tour, and also provide space for reflection. Clearly, their costs vary, depending on the destination and length of the tour. They also mean time away from the workplace. On return to the workplace, writing and disseminating a report and briefing colleagues about the trip also extend the learning opportunities.

**Case study 8.29 Discovering Dutch Libraries: Career Development
Group International Study Tour 2012**

Davis (2012) writes about her impressions of a study tour:

> I went to the Netherlands with a fascination for the country and more specifically
> Amsterdam and a real keenness to discover their libraries. I am so glad I took the
> opportunity to go on this tour, as I gained a comprehensive insight into leading
> examples of digital libraries, stunning buildings and facilities, and impressive services.
> Also, it proved to be an opportunity to be able to meet inspiring colleagues with
> whom to share experiences. As a new professional, all of this has made me feel
> hopeful for the future of libraries and information services.

SWOT analysis

Completing a SWOT analysis on an aspect of the library or information
service's teams, units, departments or activities, services and resources
provides a structured method of reflection and learning about the current
situation. A simple way to carry out a SWOT analysis is to ask a team to
complete Figure 8.2.

Strengths	Weaknesses
Opportunities	Threats (or barriers)

Figure 8.2 *SWOT analysis*

Teamwork

Teamwork is an essential part of working life and most library and information workers are members of a number of different teams. Teams which function well often have the following characteristics:

- clear goals and objectives
- clear responsibilities
- willingness to work together
- honest, open and respectful
- keep promises
- provide constructive feedback
- create a supportive environment
- celebrate success.

Activities which team leaders can introduce to help effective teamworking include:

- action planning
- use of self-assessment surveys, e.g. learning styles, teamworking styles and time management skills (for example, see Chapter 2, also www.mindtools.com)
- use of away days
- use of social events and celebrations.

Training a colleague

Training a colleague to carry out a particular activity or task benefits both the colleague, who learns a new skill, and the trainer, who gains additional experience in training. Chapter 5 provides guidance on designing and structuring a training session and Chapter 3 provides a range of different learning and teaching methods. See also Instructions earlier in this chapter.

Twitter

Twitter, a method of sending brief messages across the internet, is outlined in Chapter 4. Increasingly, individual library and information workers use it as a means of keeping up to date with developments and ideas.

Example 8.15 Twitter

Catriona Fisher (2012) writes:

> From a professional perspective, Twitter is most useful for finding out about developments in other libraries, for making contacts, for accessing publications and for following what's happening at conferences and other professional events. As well as

following the tweets for conferences from a distance, it can be very interesting to follow the tweets from an event that you're actually at – quite often you find a wide range of perspectives and interpretations of the same speech or presentation.

Video clips

It is possible to make video clips cheaply and easily using technologies such as mobile phone cameras or digital cameras, as well as more expensive kit. Thanks to the advent of YouTube, many individuals accept 'rough and ready' video clips rather than insisting on ones produced to a high 'BBC' standard.

Clearly, you need to obtain written permission from the person or people who are being videoed and explain to them how the video clip will be used (and it should not be re-purposed without their permission). Video clips can be used to enhance workplace learning in many different situations, including clips of:

- customers talking about their experiences
- senior managers expressing their support for an initiative
- specific situations, which can then form the focus of discussion in a workshop ('trigger' videos)
- demonstrations
- someone endorsing the value of a particular service or resource.

Visits

A visit to another library, library vendor or relevant organization provides an opportunity for library and information workers to:

- broaden their outlook
- gain new ideas
- compare systems and procedures
- network with other professionals.

The results of visits can be shared across the library or information service through a briefing event, report, presentation, blog or informal talk.

Case study 8.30 Library signage

Jonathan worked in a school library which was about to be refurbished. In order to gain new ideas about library signage he visited two other school libraries, a public library and also a number of large shops. Using ideas from these trips, he developed a new library signage system which made a very positive impact when the library re-opened.

Wikis

A wiki is an online tool which enables a group of people to produce a document or other collaborative output. Wikis are described in more detail in Chapter 4.

Work-based learning qualifications

Work-based learning qualifications provide opportunities to gain qualifications through development activities which are focused on the workplace. There are a wide range of work-based qualifications, which include the Qualifications and Credit Framework (QCF) qualifications, National Vocational Qualifications (NVQs), Scottish Vocational Qualifications (SVQs), Vocationally Related Qualifications (VRQs) and Technical Certificates and Apprenticeships in a wide range of subjects including:

- Advice and Guidance
- Business and Administration
- Creative and Cultural
- Libraries, Archives and Information Services
- Learning and Development
- Management.

Many library and information workers complete training qualifications in teaching and training practice, and some of these are based on practical work-based experiences.

Case study 8.31 Developing skills in learning and teaching

Thickens (2012), who works at the University of Westminster, writes about the impact of completing the Postgraduate Certificate of Special Study in Supporting Learning, which was run by his employer:

I did the course because I wanted more in-depth development than I would get through one-off training sessions or by learning on the job. My job involves running information skills training sessions with students, and I was doing this without any in-depth or current knowledge of pedagogical theory and practice, relying on presentation skills and some theory that I had picked up here and there.

The main focus of the course was on moving away from presenter-orientated sessions and encouraging students to participate actively in sessions. We were encouraged to develop our teaching throughout the course, but for me the main change came after I had finished and was able to redesign my teaching sessions to encourage more student activity.

One of the first things I did was with a member of the course team to discuss the intended learning outcomes for my session on researching for a dissertation, and to ask for a longer slot. Previously I hadn't had the confidence to do this. I also suggested preparatory reading for the students, and post-session activities to try to extend their learning. When I ran the sessions, I started by asking the students what they wanted to learn (rather than telling them what I was going to cover in the session), and I used group work and individual tasks so that they could test their own understanding. I also put much more emphasis on the feedback forms. This was something we had been encouraged to do on the course, and I have used the comments to develop a more reflective approach in this year's sessions.

At first, some of the changes that I made were not particularly subtle, but as I have become used to this way of teaching I think my practice has improved; I have used what I learnt on the course to encourage a more collegiate atmosphere in which students learn from each other as well as from me, and in which I can learn from the students. Some of this has to do with applying specific techniques such as group work, but a lot has to do with my own confidence in the role of teacher and with allowing myself to be spontaneous and developing empathy with the students. For me, this was a really important part of the course. As a result of completing the course, I enjoy the sessions I run more, and I think the students do too. The feedback has been very positive, and a good number of students comment that they like having the opportunity to ask lots of questions. This was something that I had tried to encourage before, but not so successfully.

Work shadowing

As its name suggests, work shadowing involves keeping close to someone and observing them at work. It is sometimes called 'sitting by Nellie'. Work shadowing may be used in the following learning situations:

- as part of an induction process for a new member of staff
- in training someone who has recently been promoted
- to enable different groups of staff to learn from the experiences of others.

Work shadowing is most effective if it is focused, and this means identifying the learning outcome(s) for the activity, carrying out its shadowing process, and then reflecting and debriefing on the experience. The debriefing can also be used to identify incidental or unexpected learning.

Case study 8.32 Shadowing a group of students during induction

Fiona was keen to improve the quality of the library induction events for new students. To help give her an insight into their experiences during induction she shadowed a group of students for the first three days of their induction programme. She wrote a brief report on her experiences and made a presentation to senior managers and to the team of librarians involved in induction. Following her feedback, they radically revised their programme and made the library sessions shorter, introduced games with prizes and moved much of the content onto the VLE.

Working parties

Many library and information services establish working parties or project teams in order to tackle a particular issue or problem. Working parties provide opportunities for learning for individuals, for the whole working party or team and for the library and information service as a whole.

Team leaders and managers can help to ensure that working parties and project teams promote learning by considering their membership and providing opportunities for people with less experience to learn from more experienced colleagues. Working parties can be explicitly changed into learning opportunities by ensuring that reflection and acknowledgement of learning are on the agenda for each meeting and are considered in all the project outputs (report, briefing sessions, project blog, newsletter or e-bulletins, presentations).

See also Project work.

Writing

The process of writing an article, report or book is a learning one, as it involves:

- carrying out a literature survey or original research
- organizing ideas and concepts
- writing for a particular audience.

Although some people lack confidence in their ability to write, this skill can be developed through practice, e.g. writing small entries for an e-bulletin or writing with a colleague. Some practical tips for getting started with writing include:

- Set a specific time for writing.
- Start writing – even if you are not satisfied with your work, it helps to get you going.
- Start with the topic or theme with which you are most comfortable.
- Keep it simple – avoid long and complicated sentences.
- Acknowledge that you will need to edit – all writers edit their work, so it is not a sign of failure.
- If you get stuck, then explain your idea to a colleague, friend or even a pet. This will help you to find the right form of words.
- When you think you are finished, ask a kind colleague or friend to give you feedback.
- Respond to the feedback and finish off the work.
- Send it off.

Example 8.16 Writing this book

The process of writing this book has enabled me to:

- update my knowledge of training practices
- learn about training practices in a wide range of library and information services
- update my knowledge about information and communication technologies

- review earlier books of mine and notice how the subject, my knowledge and writing skills have developed over time
- network with a wide range of library and information practitioners who have shared their experiences with me
- receive feedback from friends, colleagues and the publishing team
- enjoy the satisfaction of seeing a completed piece of work.

YouTube

YouTube provides access to an incredible range of videos. Its main advantages are that it is accessible, it is free and the videos cover a wide range of topics. However, their quality varies and it is possible to spend a lot of time searching for relevant videos. It is possible to use YouTube as a means of exploring how other libraries are providing various services, e.g. a search for library induction for university students returns examples of both good and poor (and sometimes extremely boring) practices. These could be used as a resource for a library workshop on developing student inductions.

Notes

1 schoollibrarydisplays.blogspot.co.uk.
2 For example, see www.vertext42.com/Excel/Templates/fishbone-diagram.html.
3 informationprofessionalportfolio.wordpress.com.
4 www.darkarchive.wordpress.com.
5 www.libraryservices.nhs.uk.forlibrarystaff/lqaf/.
6 www.slainte.org.uk/files/pdf/PLQIM/.

References and additional resources

Adair, J. (2005) *Effective Leadership Development*, Chartered Institute of Personnel and Development.

Allan, B. (1999) *Developing Library and Information Staff through Work-based Learning*, Facet Publishing.

Ally, M. and Needham, G. (eds) (2010) *M-Libraries 2. A virtual library in everyone's pocket*, Facet Publishing.

Ally, M. and Needham, G. (eds) (2012) *M-Libraries 3. Transforming libraries with mobile technology*, Facet Publishing.

Ayris, P. (2008) *UCL Library Services Awarded Investors in People Status*, www.ucl.ac.uk/library/iip.shtml [accessed on 24 August 2012].

Ball, K. (2010) *From Canada to Australia: arranging a library work exchange*, www.cilip.org.uk [accessed on 2 September 2012].

Baro, E. E. (2012) Job Rotation Program Evaluation: the Niger Delta University Library, *Aslib Proceedings*, **64** (4), 388–404.

Bevan, N. (2012) *Developing Your Teaching Skills*, careerdevelopment.org.uk/2012/06 [accessed on 24 August 2012].

Bloor, M., Frankland, J., Thomas, M., and Robson, K .(2001) *Focus Groups in Social Research*, Sage.

Bradley, P. (2007) *How to Use Web 2.0 in Your Library*, Facet Publishing. (Second edition to be published 2014.)

Bray, T. and Simpson, T. (2006) *A Manager's First 100 Days*, Chartered Institute of Personnel and Development.

Briscoe, J.P. and Hall, D.T. (2006) The Interplay of Boundaryless and Protean Careers: combinations and implications, *Journal of Vocational Behavior*, **69**, 4–18.

Brockband, A. and McGill, I. (2012) *Facilitating Reflective Learning*, Kogan Page.

Buzan, T. (1989) *Use Your Head*, British Broadcasting Corporation.

Clark, J. A. (2012) *Building Mobile Library Applications*, Facet Publishing.

Clifford, J. and Thorpe, S. (2007) *Workplace Learning and Development*, Kogan Page.

Clutterbuck, D. (2004) *Everyone Needs a Mentor*, 4th edn, Chartered Institute of Personnel and Development.

Clutterbuck, D. and Megginson, D. (2005) *Making Coaching Work*, Chartered Institute of Personnel and Development.

Cox, E., Bachkirova, T. and Clutterbuck, D. (2009) *The SAGE Handbook of Coaching*, Sage.

Davis, S. (2012) *Discovering Dutch Libraries: Career Development Group International Study Tour 2012*, careerdevelopmentgroup.org.uk/2012/06/ [accessed on 15 August 2012].

Dunneback, K. (2010) *Punch Up Your Portfolio*, www.liscareer.com/dunneback_portfolios.htm.

Elsegood, S. (2012) Focusing on Students' Discovery Tool Preferences, *SCONUL Focus*, **54**, 24–8.

Fee, K. (2009) *Delivering E-learning*, Kogan Page.

Fee, K. (2011) *101 Learning and Development Tools*, Kogan Page.

Fisher, C. (2012) Twitter – A Personal Perspective, *SCONUL Focus*, **54**, 51–2.

Gerding, S. (2007) *The Accidental Technology Trainer: a guide for libraries*, Independent Book Services.

Godwin, P. and Parker, J. (2008) *Information Literacy Meets Library 2.0*, Facet Publishing.

Godwin, P. and Parker, J. (2012) *Information Literacy beyond Library 2.0*, Facet Publishing.

Harding, A. (2012) Personal communication.

Herrington, J., Reeves, T. C. and Oliver, R. (2009) *A Guide to Authentic E-learning*, Routledge.

Honey, P. and Mumford, A. (1994) *101 Ways to Develop Your People Without Really Trying*, Maidenhead, Peter Honey.

Hoskins, J. (2012) *Conference Report 2*, careerdevelopmentgroup.org.uk/2012/01/conference-report-2 [accessed on 15 August 2012].

Houghton-Jan, S. (2010) *Technology Training in Libraries*, Facet Publishing.

Iverson, K. (2004) *E-learning Games*, Pearson.

Jones, G. and Gorell, R. (2012) *50 Top Tools for Coaching*, Kogan Page.

Jones, J. and Clements, P. (2008) *The Diversity Training Handbook*, Kogan Page.

Kear, K. (2010) *Online and Social Networking Communities*, Routledge.

Lampshire, J. and Lewis, L. (2008) *Coaching*, Chartered Institute of Personnel and Development.

Library and Information Health Network North West Quality Brief and Exchange Group (2011) *Examples of Key Performance Indicators for Health Libraries*, www.lihnn.nhs.uk [accessed on 15 August 2012].

Nelson, B. C. and Erlandson, B. E. (2012) *Design for Learning in Virtual Worlds*, Routledge.

Notess, G. (2012) *Screencasting for Libraries*, Facet Publishing.

Parkin, M. (2010a) *More Tales for Trainers*, Kogan Page.

Parkin, M. (2010b) *Tales for Trainers*, Kogan Page.

Parkin, M. (2010c) *Tools for Change*, Kogan Page.

Parsloe, E. and Leedham, M. (2009) *Coaching and Mentoring*, Kogan Page.

Pedler, M. (1996) *Action Learning for Managers*, Lemos and Crane.

Peltier-Davis, C. A. (2012) *The Cybrarian's Web. An A–Z guide to 101 free Web 2.0 tools and other resources*, Facet Publishing.

Ritchie, A. (2007) *Continuing Professional Development: pathways to leadership in the library and information world*, IFLA Publications.

Robinson, T. S. C. (2010) *Library Videos and Webcasts*, Facet Publishing.

Robson, F. (2009) *Effective Inductions*, Chartered Institute of Personnel and Development.

Thickens, J. (2012) Personal Communication.

Uthmann, S. (2005) Multi-skill Me. Secondment opportunities and issues at Queensland University of Technology Library. Paper presented at *2005: ALIA National Library and Information Technicians Conference*, www.eprints.qut.edu.au/20086/1/ [accessed on 1 September 2012].

Wenger, E., McDermott, R. and Snyder, W. M. (2002) *Cultivating Communities of Practice*, Harvard Business School Press.

Index

24/7 culture 2–3
360 degree feedback 154
4MAT approach 25–6, 98–9, 136, 141
70-20-10 model of workplace learning 21–2, 153

academic library, case study 5, 30, 37–9, 41, 53–8, 72–3, 76–8, 80, 82, 85, 109–10, 121, 123–6, 136–7, 143–5, 155–6, 162–3, 167, 174–5, 176, 180–1, 186, 191–12, 197, 204
accreditations 154–5
action learning 155–6
action planning 33–4, 120–1
activities 35, 119–24
advice 157–8
Allan, B. 20
ALSC (Association for Library Services to Children) 83
American Libraries 192
American Library Association 172–3
amplifier effect 22
anagrams 43
analysing mistakes 156
Anderson, L. W. 27, 28
application software *see* apps
appraisal processes 156–7
apprenticeships 121
apps 61–2, 157
ARLIS (Art Libraries Society of North America) 83
Art Libraries Society of North America 83
asking advice 157–8
assessment activity 54–5
assessment tools 197–8
Association for Library Services to Children 83
asynchronous tools 61
audience participation 50

audience response systems 63–4
audio files 64–5
audio recordings 159
Australian Library Journal 192
Ayris, P, 155

Baack, D. 108
Bachkirova, T. 184
Baker, L. 3, 41, 42
Ball, K. 173
Barker-Matthews, S. 109–10
Baro, E. E. 180
benchmarking 159–60
benefits of training 4–5
Bent, M. 65, 95
Berge, Z. 146
blended learning 133–50, 140–5
   design 141–5
blogs 65–6, 160
   case study 63
Bloom, B. S. 27–9, 96
Bloom's Taxonomy of Learning 16, 18, 27–9, 96
Bloor, M. 176
board games 41
book reviews 160–1
Boolean logic, case study 38–9
Bowen, A. 78
Bradley, P. 62, 65–6, 75
Brahmi, F. A. 64
briefing papers 161
Briscoe, J. P 185
Bruce, B. C. 48
Bush, D. A. 64
Business Balls 28
Buzan, T. 68, 186

Canadian Association for Law Librarians 83
Cann, A. 62
Carbery, A. 125
Cardiff University Library 57, 76
Career Development Group, CILIP 185

case study 200
cascade feedback 45
cascade training 161
case studies 36–7
celebrating success 161
Centre for Creative Leadership 21
Cephalonia method 57–8, 123
challenging situations
   e-learning 147–8
   face-to-face 127–30
Change Academy 196
Chartered librarian status 190
child protection 9
children's library, case study 160
CILIP 164–5, 172–3, 185, 190, 199
CILIP Update 192
Clow, K.E. 108
Clutterbuck, D. 184
coaching 162–3
college library, case study 97, 158, 166
Collins, M. 146
communities of interest 163–4
communities of practice 19–21, 163–4
competitions 164–5
complaints 165
conferences 165
   case study 161, 199
conscious competence 28–9
conscious incompetence 28–9
construction industry, example 5
content-centred training 16–17
copyright 9
corporate manslaughter 9
Costello, M. 109–10
costing staff time 8
costing training 8
course accreditation, case study 41
course design, case study 41
Cox, E. 184

crises 166
critical friend 167
Croft, K. 70
crosswords 67
CustomerFirstUK 154

data protection 9
database training 124–6
  case study 74, 141–2
Davidson, J. 48
Davies, L. 123
Davis, S. 200
deadlines 198–9
deep approach to learning 18,
  27
delegation 167–8
demonstrations 37–9, 168
design of training events 90, 95–
  100
diagnostic quiz 54
diaries see also learning journals
digital natives 3
Dimitriou, K. 62
disability issues 9, 36–7
discussion groups 39–40
discussions 120
displays 168–9
diverse groups 90–1
drop-in sessions 40–1
Dunn and Dunn model 16, 24–6
Dunn, K. 22, 24, 26
Dunn, R. 22, 24, 26
Dunneback, K. 171

e-bulletins 169
e-learning 133–50, 169 see also
  blended learning
  design 135–7
electronic mailing lists 169–70
Elsegood, S. 176
Elston, C. 136–7
e-mails 148, 170–1
  case study 37–8
Emmett, T. W. 64
employer's liability insurance 9
ending the learning process 118–
  19
engaging participants 115
English-language skills 94
English-Speaking Union 164–5
Entwistle, N. 18
e-portfolio 171–2
Equality Act 2010 91–2
e-readers 70
e-tutoring 145–8
Eva, N. 82
evaluating learning innovations,
  case study 172
evaluating products 172
evaluating training 102–7
exhibitions 173
exit interviews 173
external funding 173–4

face-to-face training 113–31
  design 97–8
FAQs see frequently asked
  questions
feedback 45, 102–7, 174–5
financial issues 8
fishbone diagram 175
Fisher, C. 121
focus groups 176
Frankland, J. 176
freedom of information 9
freelance trainers see
  independent trainers
frequently asked questions 176–
  7

games 41–3 see also playing
  cards
  case study 125–6
  internet-based tools 66–7
gap year 177
Germek, G. 79–80
Goodstein, A. 109
government library, case study
  17, 141–2, 194, 198
ground rules, e-tutoring 146
group work 44–5
  case study 45
guest speakers 45–6, 120

Hall, D. T. 185
handouts, case study 123, 125–6
hands-on sessions 46
Harding, A. 56, 90, 101, 107,
  110, 154
health and safety 9
  training 191
health library, case study 181
Hegaty, N. 97, 125
Higher Education Academy 196
holiday cover 165–6
Honey and Mumford model 16,
  24–5, 98–100
Honey, P. 22, 24, 98–9, 181
Hooley, T. 62
Hoskins, J. 199

IBL see inquiry-based learning
ice-breakers 46–7
  case study 157–8
IFLA (International Federation
  of Library Associations) 83
independent trainers 1, 9, 30,
  153–4
  case study 22–3, 56–7, 110
  marketing 110
induction 17, 178
  board game 42–3
  induction training, case study
  42–3, 55–8, 64, 70, 109,
  123–4, 136–7, 143–5, 204
information consultants, case
  study 22–3

Information Literacy Resource
  Bank 76
information skills training, case
  study 64, 76–8, 80–2, 109–
  10, 121, 123–4, 143–4,
  203–4
inquiry-based learning 47–8
instructions 178–9
intellectual property 9
interactive whiteboards 68
International Federation of
  Library Associations 83
international students 93–5
internet tools, questionnaires and
  surveys 54–5
internet-based tools, games 43
interviews 179–80
Investors in People 154–5
Ishikawa diagram 175
ISO 9000 194
IWB see interactive whiteboards

JISC 41, 69, 80–1, 91, 193–4
JISC Mail 170
JISC Netskills 80
job rotation 180–1
Joint Information Systems
  Committee see JISC
Jones, G. A. B. 72
Jones, N. 76
journals 183–4

Kahn, P. 48
Kanesho, K. N. 64
key performance indicators 7,
  181
Kirkpatrick, D. L. 89, 104, 148
Kirkpatrick model 104–7, 148–9
knowledge management, case
  study 30
Kolb, D. A. 24
KPIs see key performance
  indicators
Krathwohl, D. R. 27–8

Langan, K. 2
large groups 119–24
  case study 136–7, 129
late-comers, case study 129
law library, case study 93, 185
leadership development
  programme, case study 155–
  6
learner-centred training 18–19
learning boxes 181–2
learning communities 19–21,
  137–9
learning contracts 182–3
learning conversations 182–3
learning groups 137–9
learning journals 183–4
learning styles 16, 22–6
  case study 43

games 43
quizzes 54
lectures 49–51, 119–24
  case study 65
Leeds Metropolitan University
  71
legal issues 9
levels of competence 16, 28–9
Lewis, D. 20
LIBEX international job
  exchange programme 172–3
Library and Information Health
  Network North West 181
library guides 70
  case study 78
library staff development, case
  study 85
library tutorials 72–3
LION: Library Information
  literacy Online Network 79
literature review, case study 18–
  19
London, S. K. 64

mailing lists see electronic
  mailing lists
management and leadership
  development 21
managing groups 116, 123–4,
  127–30
marketing 107–10
marketing strategy, case study
  167
Maxwell, J. 70
McCarthy, B. 98, 141
McDermott, R. 19, 21, 163
Measday, B. 68
meetings 184
mentoring 53–4, 184–6
Mestre, L. S. 72–3
millennium generation 2–3
mind mapping 68–9, 186–7
MindTools 198
Mires, E. 57
mobile learning 69–70
Montgomery, C. 93–5
Morgan, N. 76, 123
MoRSE project 69
Moseley, A. 66
multimedia clips, case study 57–
  8
Mumford, A. 22, 24, 98–9

National Health Service Library
  Quality Assurance
  Framework 194
National Literacy Trust 83
National Student Survey 5
National Vocational
  Qualifications 121
networking 187
newsletters see e-bulletins
Nicholas, S. 76

Nicholson, H. 82
NVQs (National Vocational
  Qualifications) 121

O'Connor, J. 22
online communication tools 61
online discussion groups 187–8
online learning see also e-
  learning, blended learning
  community 20–1
  groups 137–9
online portfolio 190
online tutorial design, case study
  72–3
online tutorials 188
online voice 146
on-the-job learning experiences
  21–2
Open University 80, 93
organizing events 188–9
orientation see induction
O'Rourke, K. 48

Palgrave 95
Parkin, M. 53
participants 90–5
  with disabilities 91–3, 97
PBL see problem-based learning
PDP see personal development
  planning
Pedler, M. 155
performance management, case
  study 162–3
personal development planning
  189
personal development portfolio
  190
PhD students, case study 18–19
Pike, B. 42
plagiarism games 43, 54–5
playing cards 191
podcasts 70–1
portal see web portals
Post-it® notes see sticky notes
PowerPoint 49, 71
  activity 121
  presentations, case study 37–8
Prensky, M. 3
presentation software see
  PowerPoint
presentations 49–51, 191–2
  case study 40
  prizes 164–5
problem-based learning 51–3
professional indemnity insurance
  9
professional journals 192
professional organizations 192–3
project management training,
  case study 22–3, 193–4
project work 193–4
promoting training programmes
  107–10

promotion, career development
  194
public library, case study 30–2,
  67, 109, 129–30, 143–5,
  160, 163, 198–9
Public Library Quality
  Improvement Matrix 194

QCF (Qualifications and Credit
  Framework) 121
QR codes 72, 194
  case study 57–8
quadrant method, evaluation
  105
qualifications 203–4
Qualifications and Credit
  Framework 121
quality assurance activities 194
Queensland University of
  Technology 197
questionnaires 54–5, 74–5
questions 50–1, 117–18, 120,
  158–9
quick response codes see QR
  codes
quizzes 120–1, 195

Race, P. 105
Ralston, R. K. 64
reading 195
reasonable adjustments 91–3
Reed, L. 65
referencing skills, games 43
reflection 195–6
refreshments, case study 101
research students, case study 41
Researching Librarian 192
residentials 196
retreats 196
rich pictures 197
Richwine, M. W. 64
Ritchie, A. 197
RNIB 93
Robson, K. 176
role play 168

SAFARI 80
Salmon. G. 137, 139, 149
Savin-Baden, M. 52
scavenger hunts 55–6
Schneider, M. 136–7
school library, case study 56–7,
  68, 72, 107, 202
Scopes, M. 70
Scottish Library and Information
  Council 194
Scottish Vocational
  Qualifications 121
screen recording 72–3
screen sharing 74
  case study 82
secondment 197
self-assessment tools 197–8

self-employed trainers *see*
    independent trainers
self-paced tutorials *see* online
    tutorials
self-service system training 30
Seymour, J. 22
shadowing 204
signage, case study 202
Skills@Library 81, 137
Skills4Study 95
Skills in Accessing, Finding and
    Reviewing Information
    (SAFARI) 80
Skopelja, E. N. 86
Skype 3, 45, 78, 81–2 *see also*
    web conferencing
    case study 82
SMART action plan 33–4
smartboard *see* interactive
    whiteboards
Smith, A. L. 3, 41, 42
Snyder, W. 19, 21, 163
social learning 19–21
social media 61–62
social networking tools 2–3, 74,
    83–4
Solem, L. 42
special library *see* workplace
    library
speed networking 199
squiggle game 43
staff development 153–208
staff exchanges 172–3
stakeholders 7
starting training sessions 113–15
Stevenson, P. 106
sticky notes 199
stories 53–4
    case study 30–1
strategic plan 3–4
student helpers, case studies
    158, 177
study skills
    case study 70–1
    quizzes 55
study tours 199–200
Sugar, S. 42
surface approach to learning 18,
    27
Survey Monkey 74

surveys 54–5, 74–5
SVQs (Scottish Vocational
    Qualifications) 121
Swain, E. 76
SWOT analysis 200
synchronous tools 61

Teacher Librarian 192
teamwork 201
technical certificates 121
technology-enhanced learning
    61–85
TED talks 78
teenagers, case study 109
Texas State Library and Archives
    Commission 83
theories of learning 22–30
Thickens, J. 121
Thomas, M. 176
time management, case study
    198
timing of training sessions 100–
    2, 125
trainer-centred training 16–17
training
    colleagues 201
    interventions 116
    styles 99–100
training cycle 1, 5–6
training needs analysis 6–7
training plan 7–8
train-the-trainer 85
    case study 20–1, 40, 45
treasure hunts 55–6, 70, 72
turning point 63
tutor-centred training 16–17
Twitter 75, 201–2

unconscious competence 28–9
unconscious incompetence 28–9
University College Dublin 190
University College London 155
University of Auckland 79
University of Leeds 81, 137
University of Westminster 57–8,
    121
Uthmann, S. 197

VAK model 16, 22–4, 30
video clips 202

videoconferencing 45, 78
videos 76
virtual learning environments
    61, 76–7
    case study 37–8
virtual talks 78
virtual visitor 45–6, 78
visits 202
visual, auditory, kinaesthetic
    model 16, 22–4
VLE *see* virtual learning
    environments
Vocationally Related
    Qualifications 121
voluntary organization library,
    case study 160, 166
VRQs (Vocationally Related
    Qualifications) 121

Waterford Institute of
    Technology 125
Web 2.0 3, 61, 66–7, 83–4
web conferencing 81–2
web portals 83–4
web-based training 61, 78–81,
    135–7
Webber, S. 65
webinars 82–3
weblog *see* blogs
welcome space, case study 57–8
Wenger, E. 19, 21, 163
Whipple, E. 64
Whitton, N. 66
wikis 84–5, 202–3
work shadowing 204
work-based learning
    qualifications 203–4
working parties 204–5
workplace learning 11, 153–208
workplace learning programmes
    21–2
workplace library, case study 82,
    109, 135, 157–8, 193–4
writing 205–6

YouTube 78, 206